$14.99

HEADLINE SERIES

Nos. 333–334   FOREIGN POLICY

D0685158

The Persian Gulf
Tradition and Transformation

Cover image: NASA/Photo Researchers
The Persian Gulf, at center, and Western Asia pictured in a satellite image from the MODIS sensors on the Terra and Aqua satellites. Regions in brown indicate deserts.

Author

LAWRENCE G. POTTER *is Deputy Director of Gulf/2000, a major research and documentation project on the Persian Gulf states based at Columbia University, where he is Adjunct Associate Professor of International Affairs. A graduate of Tufts College, he received an M.A. in Middle Eastern Studies from the University of London, and a Ph.D. in history from Columbia. He taught in Iran for four years before the revolution. From 1984 to 1992 he was Senior Editor at the Foreign Policy Association and currently serves on FPA's Editorial Advisory Committee. He specializes in the history of Iran and the Persian Gulf and U.S. policy toward the Middle East. In addition to articles and edited volumes on the region, he edited and wrote an introduction to* The Persian Gulf in History *(Palgrave Macmillan, 2009).*

Acknowledgments

The author would like to express his sincere gratitude to colleagues who offered valuable insights and corrections to an earlier draft of this book. These include F. Gregory Gause III, who kindly reviewed the entire manuscript, as well as Ali Ansari, Farideh Farhi, Michael Izady, Phebe Marr, Gerd Nonneman, Lila Noury, Jalil Roshandel, Jean-François Seznec and Gary Sick. Naturally they do not bear any responsibility for the opinions presented in the text.

The Foreign Policy Association

The Foreign Policy Association is a private, nonprofit, nonpartisan educational organization. Its purpose is to stimulate wider interest and more effective participation in, and greater understanding of, world affairs among American citizens. Among its activities is the continuous publication, dating from 1935, of the HEADLINE SERIES. The author is responsible for factual accuracy and for the views expressed. FPA itself takes no position on issues of U.S. foreign policy. In keeping with FPA style, sources are not footnoted, but the author will be happy to supply references if requested.

HEADLINE SERIES (ISSN 0017-8780) is published occasionally by the Foreign Policy Association, Inc., 470 Park Avenue South, New York, NY 10016. Chairman, Archibald Cox, Jr.; President, Noel V. Lateef; Editor in Chief, Karen M. Rohan; Assistant Editor, Leslie Huang. Single copy price $8.99; double issue $14.99; special issue $12.99. Discount 15% on 10 to 99 copies; 20% on 100 and over. Payment must accompany all orders. Second-class postage paid at New York, NY, and additional mailing offices. POSTMASTER: Send address changes to HEADLINE SERIES, Foreign Policy Association, 470 Park Avenue South, New York, NY 10016. Copyright 2011 by Foreign Policy Association, Inc. Printed at The Sheridan Press, Hanover, PA. Published Fall 2011.

Library of Congress Control Number: 2011934233
ISBN: 978-0-87124-234-1

Introduction

THE PERSIAN GULF is one of the most critical flash points in the world today. After a revolution and three major wars in the past 30 years, the Gulf's continued strategic significance is not in doubt. The future political trajectory of the region, however, is uncertain and all the Gulf states believe themselves to be in a vulnerable position. It has been said that the Gulf is a region of strong enemies, weak friends and vital interests. Tensions there are dangerously high, and neighboring states' trust in each other—a prerequisite for defusing problems—is clearly lacking.

Ever since the Iran-Iraq War (1980–88), with the unrestrained mutual disparagement of Sunni and Shi'i and Arab and Persian, the discourse in the region has served to inflame sectarian tensions. Gulf Arabs are very nervous about Iran's intentions, and the documents released by the whistle-blower Web site WikiLeaks quoted leaders of Saudi Arabia, Qatar and the United Arab Emirates (UAE) urging the United States to get tough—the Saudi king, referring to Iran, reportedly advised the U.S. to "cut off the head of the snake." In the future, Gulf monarchies will be concerned about Iraq's intentions, and there are already renewed tensions between Iraq and Kuwait.

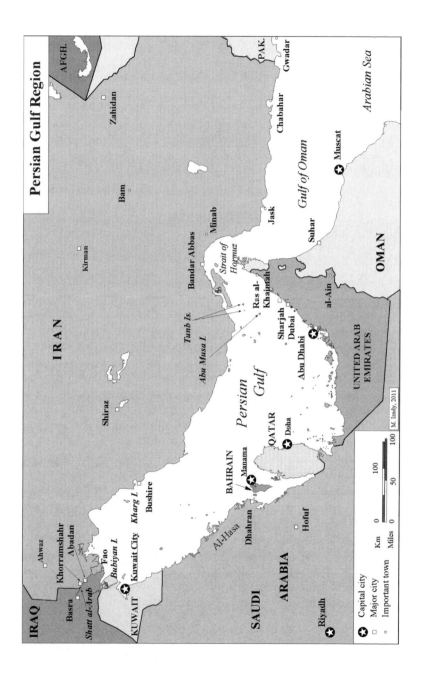

Persian Gulf Region

AFGH.

IRAN

Zahidan

Bam

Kirman

Shiraz

Bushire

Kharg I.

Ahwaz

Khorramshahr
Abadan

Basra

Fao

Shatt al-Arab

Bubiyan I.

Kuwait City

KUWAIT

Bandar Abbas

Strait of
Hormuz

Minab

Jask

Tunb Is.

Abu Musa I.

Ras al-
Khaimah

Sharjah
Dubai

Abu Dhabi

al-Ain

UNITED ARAB
EMIRATES

OMAN

Suhar

Muscat

Gulf of Oman

Arabian Sea

Chabahar

Gwadar

PAK.

Persian

Gulf

QATAR

Doha

BAHRAIN

Manama

Dhahran

Al-Hasa

Hofuf

SAUDI

ARABIA

Riyadh

★ Capital city
□ Major city
○ Important town

Km   0   100

Miles 0   50   100

M. Izady, 2011

Although historically important as a trade route linking east and west, the present importance of the Gulf stems from its massive energy deposits. Fifty-four percent of the world's proven oil reserves are located in the Gulf countries. (By comparison, North America holds 5.3%.) Gulf oil now accounts for about 17% of U.S. imports and 16% of Europe's, but the figure for Japan is 84%. China gets more than a quarter of its oil from the Gulf and is a major investor in the oil sector in both Iran and Iraq. Protecting this oil is very expensive, and this has prompted American complaints that other countries do not make a fair contribution to the defense of the Gulf.

The Arab awakening that has swept the Middle East since early 2011 has had a cataclysmic effect in the region, and continued upheaval is likely. The pro-democracy uprisings reflected the challenge of a new generation and in the Gulf inspired petitions demanding change, as well as public protests in Saudi Arabia, Bahrain and Oman. Gulf rulers have responded to demands for political reform by blaming Iran and seeking to buy off potential opposition; they also resorted to repression in Saudi Arabia, the UAE and Kuwait, and violent crackdowns in Bahrain and Oman. "It's safe to say that— at least for now—the Gulf region is becoming more repressive, not less, with potentially dangerous long-term consequences not only for these oil-rich monarchies but also for their Western allies," in the opinion of Dr. Kristian Coates Ulrichsen of the London School of Economics (LSE). People in the Middle East, as well as policymakers in Washington, wonder if a new political order is forming. Because of the long-term stagnation in Egypt and in Iraq, until recently many people regarded the center of gravity in the Middle East as shifting to the Gulf—but now it may shift back back to Egypt.

The Persian Gulf

The Persian Gulf is a 600-mile-long arm of the Indian Ocean that separates the Arabian peninsula from Iran. (Since the 1950s Arab states have referred to it as the Arabian Gulf, in an attempt to give it a new identity and belittle Iran.) The Gulf is bordered by Iran and seven Arab states: Iraq, Kuwait, Saudi Arabia, Bahrain, Qatar, the UAE and Oman. It is bounded by the Shatt al-Arab waterway in the north, which forms the frontier between Iran and Iraq, and the Strait of Hormuz in the south, which connects it to the Gulf of Oman and the Indian Ocean. The strait, which is 34 miles wide at its narrowest point, is the choke point of the Gulf: 40% of all oil traded by sea moves through it. In 2010, about 15.5 million barrels of oil were transported out of the Gulf every day on supertankers. The possibility of its closure by Iran has been a nightmare for Western defense planners since the Iranian revolution.

In mid-2011, the eight littoral states contained some 155 million people, representing many ethnic, religious, linguistic and political communities. In 1950, their combined population was estimated to be around 24 million; it is projected to rise to 197 million by the year 2025. This population is unevenly distributed, with Iran, Iraq and Saudi Arabia together accounting for 138.5 million. All of the Gulf states must contend with young and rapidly rising populations. (In Iran, for example, a population of 35 million at the time of the revolution in 1978 has swollen to 78 million.)

Muslims are split into two major sects, Sunni and Shi'i. The two differ over who was legitimately entitled to lead the Islamic community after the death of the Prophet Muhammad in A.D. 632. Sunnis predominate; they believe that the community should choose its own leader. Shi'is, who are a majority in Iran, Iraq and Bahrain, believe leadership is vested in the family of the Prophet. Sunni Islam has historically been associated with bestowing legitimacy on the power of rulers; Shi'i Islam, with opposition, martyrdom and revolt.

The majority of Iranians were converted to Shi'ism in the 16th and 17th centuries. Although southern Iraq and the holy cities of Najaf and Karbala have always been the Shi'i heartland, Iraq only became majority Shi'i in the 19th century. A Shi'i community existed in Bahrain and eastern Arabia (al-Hasa) from about the 10th century, but since the rise of the Wahhabi movement in Arabia in the mid-18th century, and particularly since the formation of the state of Saudi Arabia in 1932, Shi'is there have come under heavy pressure.

Since the revolution in Iran in 1978–79 and the rise of Shi'is

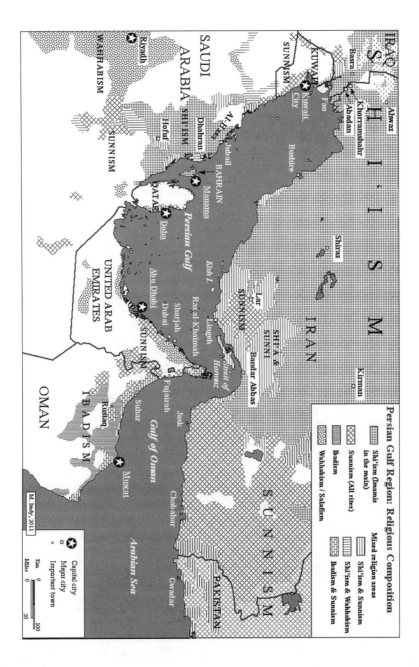

Persian Gulf Region: Religious Composition

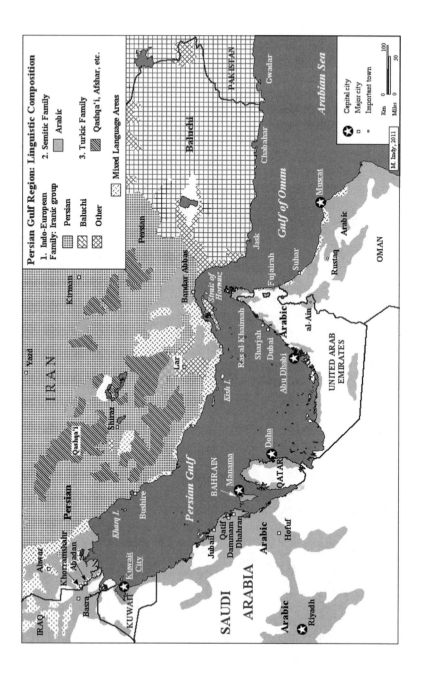

Persian Gulf Region: Linguistic Composition

1. Indo-European Family: Iranic group
- Persian
- Baluchi
- Other

2. Semitic Family
- Arabic

3. Turkic Family
- Qashqa'i, Afshar, etc.

Mixed Language Areas

★ Capital city
□ Major city
○ Important town

Km 0   50   100
Mi 0   50

M. Izady, 2011

in Lebanon in the 1970s, Shi'ism has been regarded as a powerful political force that can mobilize the downtrodden and pose a challenge to ruling regimes. By the late 20th century some Shi'i-majority countries that had Sunni governments—such as Iraq and Bahrain—witnessed the rise of resistance movements. Most outsiders associate Shi'ism with its Iranian version and have underestimated the countervailing force of nationalism, as demonstrated among Iraqis during their war with Iran in the 1980s.

Another major cleavage pits Arab against Persian. Arabic, a Semitic language, is spoken in Iraq and the states of the peninsula. Iran has an Aryan heritage, and its main language, Persian (Farsi), is an Indo-European tongue. Persians regard their cultural legacy as richer than that of the Arabs, although their religion, Islam, was founded by an Arab, the Prophet Muhammad.

Persian Gulf security

The security of the Persian Gulf has been a concern of outside powers for the past 500 years, and the situation today resembles that which has long prevailed: an imperial hegemon—now the U.S.—tries to maintain stability thanks to naval superiority and an alliance with key regional states. However, the U.S. has never been able to exert complete control over these states nor prevent local rivalries.

With the implosion of Iraq in 2003, the strategic configuration in the region changed overnight, as one leg of the political triangle—Iran, Iraq and the six Gulf Cooperation Council (GCC) states: Saudi Arabia, Kuwait, Qatar, Bahrain, the UAE and Oman—that dominated regional affairs suddenly collapsed. Iraq had traditionally served as a balance to Iran and a bulwark against Iranian expansion. Saudi Arabia was a lesser counterweight. The rise of a Shi'i-dominated government in Iraq, coupled with the belligerent rhetoric of the Ahmadinejad regime in Iran and its accelerated nuclear program, has unnerved Sunni-ruled Gulf states. There is now serious tension between Iran and Saudi Arabia, which amounts to a new cold war in the Gulf. According to Prof. Abdullah Al Shayji of Kuwait University, the Iranian design is to "intimidate, co-opt and dominate" the Gulf, and "the GCC states are hapless bystanders and mute witnesses to the showdown between the Americans and the Iranians...."

Above all, in the Gulf there is an intertwining of internal and external security challenges. This is illustrated by ongoing conflicts in Bahrain and Yemen, seen by some as proxy wars between Iran and Saudi Arabia. The impact of globalization and media penetration of the region, the widespread availability of information and the growing youth bulge, all presage a new kind of politics in which ruling elites increasingly have to respond to the wishes of their citizens. This became glaringly evident in the recent demonstrations of "people power" that have swept the Middle East.

The U.S. role

For the past several decades the U.S. has been the predominant military power in the Gulf. Since the Carter Administration declared in 1980 that the U.S. was determined to prevent any outside power from taking control of the Gulf, Washington has regarded the region as vital to its economic and strategic interests. It has gone to war against Iraq twice to protect those interests. What to do about Iran has been a conundrum for U.S. Administrations for the past quarter century.

Since World War II the main U.S. goal in the region has been to safeguard access to Gulf oil and to prevent any other power (first the Soviet Union and later Iraq and Iran) from threatening this. The Gulf states also figure in a number of other American foreign policy concerns, including terrorism, the spread of weapons of mass destruction (WMDs), radical Islam, democratization, human rights and the Arab-Israeli peace process. The U.S. is now preoccupied with winding down the war in Iraq, which began in 2003.

U.S. primacy partly depends on close cooperation with friendly Arab governments, especially the six GCC states. Without U.S. protection, the Gulf monarchies would find it harder to resist pressure from Iran and Iraq. A key unknown factor is the continued willingness of the U.S. to serve as the protector, and, in effect, regulator of the Gulf, and whether it will be welcome to do so. The Obama Administration plans to reduce its military involvement in the region, and this is demanded by American public opinion. Yet other countries are not stepping in to help. Although U.S. forces are scheduled to leave Iraq soon, Baghdad will need U.S. military assistance for a long time. Gulf monarchies are not confident that the U.S. will protect them, but have no one else to turn to.

The downfall of the pro-American leader in Tunisia in January 2011, followed in February by the dramatic collapse of the government of Hosni Mubarak in Egypt, had a galvanizing effect on Arab opinion. Reverberations continue throughout the region, with the departure of the Yemeni president in June, the flight of Muamar Qadhafi in August and ongoing strife in Bahrain, necessitating a reevaluation of policies on the part of the U.S. and its allies in the Persian Gulf. American influence there is widely regarded as being at a low point, with Saudi Arabia feeling betrayed by the U.S. allowing Mubarak, a fellow Sunni ruler, to fall. The Obama Administration so far has been unable to strike a deal with Iran over its nuclear program, advance the peace process between Palestinians and Israelis or turn the tide in Afghanistan.

Formulating an effective policy to assure the security of the Persian Gulf has not been easy for the U.S. Up until the attacks of 9/11, Washington had been satisfied with maintaining the status quo, even permitting Iraqi President Saddam Hussein to remain in power after Iraq had been defeated in war. However, in a major change of approach, in 2003 President George W. Bush waged a preventive war against Iraq in a bid to overthrow Saddam and install democracy. It has not turned out that way, and President Barack Obama has been severely tested in trying to bring two wars initiated by the Bush Administration to a satisfactory conclusion. In addition, by mid-2011 the U.S. found itself embroiled in civil war in Libya and political upheaval in Yemen. The killing of Osama bin Laden on May 2 was a boost to morale, but many analysts noted that al-Qaeda had already declined as a threat, and political Islam was not a factor in the revolts. The U.S. is conflicted in formulating policy toward the region as it has to weigh its support for democracy with that for autocratic leaders with whom it has long worked to preserve "stability." It is certain that the Gulf will remain a key challenge for policymakers in the future.

Conclusion

Because Gulf security has been provided by outsiders for so long, regional states rarely take the initiative. The situation that prevails there today, though, seems unsustainable over the long term. As the U.S. reduces its footprint, the littoral states, especially the triangle of interests represented by Iran, Iraq and the GCC, will inevitably and increasingly determine the course of events. It is necessary to think about a future security regime in the Gulf in which outsiders play a much smaller role and the Gulf states themselves take on more responsibility for their own security.

The Gulf is a region in which transnational forces and contested loyalties—ethnic, linguistic, and religious—continue to play a prominent role, and that occasionally leads to disputes. However, regional states have lived with such tensions for a long time, and they will not necessarily lead to conflict. Adversaries such as Iran and Saudi Arabia have in the past cooperated to achieve common goals such as higher oil prices. It is important to keep in mind that the Gulf states are locked in a state of mutual dependence that will not change.

$$\Longrightarrow \circ \Longleftarrow$$

In order to provide a better appreciation of this critical region and the future challenges it faces, this double HEADLINE SERIES will briefly review the Gulf's historical legacy and the transformation of traditional societies into modern states following the discovery of oil. It then will examine the impact and significance of three major wars in the Gulf since 1980 and describe the challenges facing the GCC states, as well as Iran and Iraq. A final chapter will discuss U.S. policy toward the region.

1

From Traditional to Modern States

THE PERSIAN GULF, while important as an international trade route connecting the Middle East to Africa, India and China, has its own distinct cultural identity. The Gulf has historically been an integrated region characterized by constant interchange of people, commerce and religious movements. Before the modern era, peoples of the region shared a maritime culture based on pearling, fishing and long-distance trade, and many tribes moved freely back and forth. This led to an intermingling of linguistic and religious communities, with many Arabic speakers and Sunni Muslims on the Persian side of the Gulf, and a Shi'i, Persian-speaking community on the Arab side.

In the past, regional powers rarely exercised effective political control over the Gulf littoral. Because of physical impediments such as mountains and deserts, peoples living on the shores of the Gulf historically had closer relations with each other than with those living in the interior. In the 19th century, they had little to do with the primary regional powers, the Persian and the Ottoman empires and the paramount shaikhs in Arabia, all of which had capitals inland. People in the coastal towns were, however, part of an interlinked system that included agricultural villages and oases that sustained the caravan trade.

Maritime society in the Gulf

The Gulf's orientation was outward, and its sailors maintained close ties with the Indian subcontinent and East Africa. A cosmopolitan, mercantile and tolerant society developed there and thrived in trade, despite the lack of local resources. A well-organized Arab dhow trade frequented ports along these coasts: for example, ships would load up with dates from Basra, in southern Iraq, and sail down to Africa in the fall on the northeast monsoon, peddling the dates and whatever else they could trade, such as salt and rice. They returned on the southwest monsoon with mangrove poles from Africa for construction and teak, coir (coarse coconut fiber) and shipbuilding materials from India. In addition to their cargoes, the dhows were always packed with passengers, including pilgrims to the holy cities of Mecca and Medina. Dhow transport was very cheap (the sailors received no pay, only a share in the meager profits), perfectly suited to the climate and provided storage at the destination until the goods could be sold. As recently as the eve of World War II, there were an estimated 2,000 vessels with 30,000–40,000 sailors engaged in such trade in the ports of the Arabian peninsula.

During the summer months, when the dhows could not sail southward because of adverse winds, activity focused on the pearl beds, the most valuable resource of the Gulf before oil. Pearling was very much a seasonal occupation, taking place from June through September when the surface temperature of the water was around 85° F. Pearls were found throughout much of the Gulf, with the best ones taken from waters northeast of Bahrain. Most were sent to Bombay for sale. With the introduction of Japanese cultured pearls in the 1930s, the bottom dropped out of the market, and many former pearlers went to work in the nascent oil industry.

14

This illustration circa 1870 depicts pearl divers in the Persian Gulf holding their breath as they dive to the seabed on lines in search of natural pearls.

Tribes and state formation

In addition to a maritime heritage, the peoples on the Gulf's southern shore also have a common legacy of tribal rule that originated in the interior of Arabia. Because of the lack of water, most tribesmen were pastoral nomads who were constantly migrating to sustain themselves and their herds of camels, sheep and goats. (In contrast to the Bedouins of Arabia, Iranian tribes that wintered near the Gulf usually migrated to the highlands in summer and back again for the winter.)

As in many parts of the premodern Middle East, society in the Arabian peninsula was tribally organized. Anthropologists, however, have not been able to agree on a definition for the word "tribe." Tribal people may view themselves very differently than outsiders do, especially governments. Kinship and patrilineal descent, real or imagined, are usually important aspects of a tribe's social structure, as is an egalitarian ideal. The power, cohesion and even identity of a tribe can change, with new ones being formed and older ones disintegrating.

Traditionally, tribal leadership was vested in a shaikh, but his authority was only as first among equals. The shaikh's authority was provisional, and dissatisfied tribesmen could replace or assassinate him—in the 19th century, ruling shaikhs in the Gulf were frequently overthrown. It was not unusual for populations unhappy with a shaikh to move elsewhere en masse, especially in the Gulf ports, where boats and not land constituted capital. For example, in 1910 a group of leading pearl merchants in Kuwait, objecting to new taxes imposed by the ruler, took up residence in Bahrain in protest. The shaikh had to give in and cancel the taxes, since he could not do without the revenues the merchants provided.

Typical tribal institutions were the *majlis*, or public audience, where anyone could approach the ruler to seek redress of his problems, and the process of *shura*, or consultation. In a consultative form of government, the leading shaikh ruled with the cooperation of his kinsmen and prominent merchants. If one shaikh was overthrown, another member of his family usually assumed power, since legitimacy to rule was reckoned to run in families. The tribal ethos has helped ensure the long rule of family dynasties in the Persian Gulf.

Tribes were the key to forming modern states in the Arabian peninsula; the dynasties presently ruling there are all of tribal origin. (In the 19th century, tribes also played an important political role in Persia and Ottoman Iraq.) Particularly significant was a religious reform movement known as Wahhabism, which arose in the central region of Najd in the eighteenth century. It was founded by Muhammad b. Abd al-Wahhab (d.1792), a preacher who formed a partnership in 1744 with a local chieftain, Muhammad b. Sa'ud (d. 1765), and went on to conquer much of the peninsula. The Wahhabi version of Islam is austere: it seeks a return to a purified faith and opposes all "innovations," such as saint worship and Shi'ism.

Possibly because of drought in the interior, many tribes at this time moved to the Gulf coast, with the Al Sabah family establishing itself in Kuwait and the Al Khalifa in Bahrain. The Al Thani had taken over Qatar by the late 1800s. The migration to the coast and the growth of towns, such as Kuwait, Bahrain, Abu Dhabi and Dubai, marked an important development in Gulf society. It led to the stronger identification of a tribe with a particular geographical location and helped to strengthen the authority of the ruler. The precarious balance of power between the nomadic Bedouins and the settled communities began to shift in favor of the latter. Increased urbanization also led to greater contact with the outside world. The British did not suppress tribalism in the Gulf, but they profoundly altered its character by giving the shaikhs under their protection the means to exert more autocratic control over their followers.

British paramountcy

Before the discovery of oil, the Gulf was a backwater noted mainly for its infernal climate. The modern strategic importance of the Gulf dates from the mid-19th century, when three great empires confronted each other there: British India, Tsarist Russia and Ottoman Turkey. The British established political control over much of the Gulf in the early 1800s and kept it for 150 years, establishing a tradition of outside involvement that persists today.

European powers' intervention in the Gulf starting in the early 1800s decisively influenced the political evolution of the Gulf states. The maritime warfare (characterized as "piracy" by Europeans) that flourished in the Gulf was a menace to their trade and communications, and the African slave trade was an affront to their sensibilities. The British interest, which at first was primarily commercial, was increasingly bound up with concern for the defense of India and subsequently a determination to exclude other powers, especially Russia.

British policy toward the Gulf and the states surrounding it was formulated by authorities in England and in India, which often resulted in confusion. The Foreign Office in London was chiefly concerned with maintaining its European alliances and not provoking Russia and the Ottomans. The India Office, which represented the authorities in Bombay and Calcutta, resented being obliged to subsidize Gulf security while often being overruled on policy. British diplomats assigned to the Gulf were members of the Indian Political Service, and, as described by Dr. James Onley of the University of Exeter, they instituted a system of indirect rule identical to the one they had developed in India. Britain's policy in the Gulf did not unfold according to a grand plan but, due to the slowness of communications, was often the result of actions taken by local officials that their government later had to support.

Britain initially brought peace to the waters of the Gulf by establishing what became known as the trucial system. In 1835, it persuaded the shaikhs in the lower Gulf to sign a treaty promising to abstain from warfare during the pearling season. Any infraction was to be punished by the British Navy. This worked well and was renewed annually until it was made permanent in 1853. The so-called Pirate Coast was now referred to as the Trucial Coast, the area that today comprises the UAE.

Britain wanted to avoid establishing formal protectorates in the Gulf—it could not afford them and did not want to get bogged down in regulating the internal affairs of littoral states. In 1861, however, it recognized the independence of Bahrain and pledged to protect it from external aggression. (Since Bahrain was an island, its protection could be assured by British naval power.) Later Britain concluded a number of exclusive agreements with other Gulf shaikhs, guaranteeing them protection in return for control over their foreign policy. This became more urgent after 1871, when the Ottomans occupied the al-Hasa region on the Arabian coast south of Kuwait. France and Russia also became more active in the Gulf in the 1880s and 1890s, which further alarmed Britain.

In 1891, Britain entered into an exclusive agreement with the sultan of Muscat and Oman under which the ruler agreed (in a "nonalienation clause") not to cede, sell or mortgage any portion of his territory to any foreign power except Britain. The following year, Britain signed similar agreements with the Trucial shaikhs, who promised not to enter into agreements with any other power, nor permit another power, without British permission, to station a resident diplomat or yield control of any part of their territory. Qatar was brought into this system in 1916.

For most of the 19th century, the British considered Kuwait to be a dependency of the Ottomans. Ottoman influence in Kuwait increased after their invasion of al-Hasa, and the ruling shaikh of Kuwait rendered a nominal tribute and accepted an Ottoman title. However, the Ottoman government in Basra intervened little in Kuwaiti affairs. In 1896, the ruler was murdered by his half-brother, Shaikh Mubarak Al Sabah, who seized power and appealed to the British for protection. In 1899 they agreed to guarantee his rule and that of his descendants in return for a nonalienation clause and the control of foreign relations. In an unratified accord of 1913, the British recognized Kuwait (defined to include Bubiyan and Warba islands) as an autonomous district of the Ottoman Empire, while the Ottomans accepted the 1899 agreement. At the outbreak of World War I in 1914, Kuwait was recognized as an independent state under British protection.

The circumstances under which Shaikh Mubarak exercised power illustrate how British involvement changed the nature of shaikhly authority. After Britain pledged to support him, Mubarak built a new palace, bought a yacht and automobile, and raised his salute from five guns to twelve—one fewer than the British Resident. In a similar manner, shaikhs throughout the Gulf, who previously had ruled in consultation with their tribesmen and the merchants, became increasingly autocratic. As noted by historian Frederick Anscombe, although "the British records give a misleading impression of weak, squabbling rulers," they actually played off the imperial powers very astutely. The British treated the shaikhs they dealt with as rulers *(hakim)* over the settled urban populations—which exceeded the prerogatives of a shaikh as traditionally understood—and held them accountable for the actions of their inhabitants. Upon independence, they would assume the grander title of *amir*, often used for military commanders and princes.

By curtailing smuggling and the profitable slave and arms trade, the British also altered the traditional economy of the Gulf. Euro-

A native dhow with full sail passes an oil tanker tied up at the British-owned Anglo-Iranian Oil Company docks in Abadan, Iran, on June 28, 1951.

pean steamships provided regular service between Bombay and the Gulf ports after 1862, and the opening of the Suez Canal in 1869 led to more frequent service with Europe. Europeans took over most of the long-distance trade (which increased the importance of a few major ports such as Basra, Bushire and Mohammerah), while relegating native dhows to the peddlar trade in smaller ports. Local businessmen now became agents for goods manufactured in Europe as the Gulf was increasingly integrated into the world economy.

Boundary drawing and the question of borders

After World War I, the political map of much of the Middle East was redrawn. The Ottoman Empire was replaced by modern states, including Turkey, Iraq and Saudi Arabia; Tsarist Russia, by the Soviet Union. The small Arab shaikhdoms on the western shore of the Gulf were under British protection until 1971 (in the case of Kuwait, 1961). Iran was never a colony, and for most of the 19th and 20th centuries, Britain competed with Russia for influence there.

The dissolution of the Ottoman Empire after World War I put the victors in war, principally Britain and France, in charge of dividing up the former enemy territories. The Persian boundaries had already been largely settled. During the second half of the 19th century, the government in Tehran retook the Arab principalities strung out along its southern coast from Bushire to the border of India and reintegrated them into the Iranian nation. Khuzistan, the southwest province, was finally subdued by Reza Shah in 1924.

Determining the exact boundaries in the Arabian peninsula, however, had not been considered very important and was opposed by local rulers. Part of the problem was conceptual: the idea that sovereignty was linked to territory was a European one. In Arabia, traditionally loyalty was given to a leader, not to a geographic entity. A shaikh held sovereignty over his tribe, wherever they roamed throughout their *dirah*, or grazing area. A tribe's location could change depending on the weather, and an arbitrary boundary in the desert could not constrain their migrations.

With the establishment of Iraq as a British mandate in 1920, the British had to draw a border between the new state, the Saudi region of Najd and Kuwait. The new boundary left Iraq with only 36 miles of frontage on the Persian Gulf, and its main port of Basra, located 75 miles upriver, was the only outlet for a virtually landlocked country. Kuwait, on the other hand, had one of the best harbors on the Gulf and 310 miles of coastline. A further annoyance was that in order to reach its small port of Umm Qasr, Iraqi vessels had to pass by or through Kuwaiti waters near the islands of Bubiyan and Warba. Since the late 1930s Iraq has tried to acquire these islands, for without them it will never feel secure about access to its own coastline.

There has also been a longstanding dispute between Iran and

Iraq (and before this the Persian and Ottoman empires) over the Shatt al-Arab, the waterway formed by the confluence of the Tigris, Euphrates and Karun rivers that forms their common border. Under an 1847 treaty that was reaffirmed in 1937, the entire river up to the Iranian shore (except for short stretches opposite Abadan and Mohammarah) was considered Iraqi territory. Iran, however, since the 1930s has sought to follow the principle of the *thalweg*, that is, the division of the river at the point of its deepest navigable channel. This was finally agreed to by Iraq in 1975.

The dispute over the sovereignty of Abu Musa and the two Tunb islands, one of the most serious flash points today, also originated in the late 19th century. Their value is primarily strategic: they are located in the shipping lanes near the Strait of Hormuz and in modern times have served as bases for Iran's Islamic Revolutionary Guard Corps (IRGC or Revolutionary Guard). Evidence for ownership of the islands before the 19th century is inconclusive, but by the late 1800s Persia had laid claim to all of them on the basis that it had owned them before the British arrived, and that in the 1880s the islands had paid tribute to Persia.

However, the Arab ruler of Sharjah also claimed Abu Musa, and the ruler of Ras al-Khaimah, the Tunbs. Their position was backed by the British government, which wanted the islands to be controlled by shaikhs under its influence and not that of Persia. A compromise solution proposed by Iran in the 1930s to give Abu Musa to Sharjah and the Tunbs to Iran was never implemented. In 1971, as the British withdrew from the Gulf, Iran seized the Tunbs and forced Sharjah to agree to share sovereignty over Abu Musa.

Oil and social change

The story of the Persian Gulf in the 20th century is the story of oil. It is really two stories: the exploration, discovery and export of petroleum on the one hand, and the effect this had on traditional societies on the other. The vast revenues that suddenly accrued to the fortunate Gulf states have led to far-reaching economic changes, but, on the Arabian peninsula, few political ones. Indeed, as will be

A satellite image shows the Shatt al-Arab (River of the Arabs) in the Persian Gulf. The southern end constitutes the Iran-Iraq border and has been at the center of disputes between the two countries.

shown, the oil revenues coupled with British support enabled monarchies, such as those that were overthrown in most other Middle Eastern states after World War II, to persist in the Gulf.

Oil was first discovered in southwest Iran at Masjid-i Sulaiman in 1908. In 1914, on the eve of World War I, the British government (which needed an assured supply of oil for its warships) assumed control of its producer, the Anglo-Persian Oil Company. Oil was discovered in commercial quantities in Iraq at Kirkuk (in the Kurdish region) in 1927; in Bahrain in 1932; and in Saudi Arabia and Kuwait in 1938. Before World War II, Iran was the leading oil exporter in the Middle East, and its refinery at Abadan was the largest in the world. Major exports from the Arab side did not begin until after World War II.

Oil operations in a country were usually controlled exclusively by a single operating company, often a joint venture or partnership. Such arrangements discouraged competition, and companies colluded to prevent overproduction, which would lower prices. Britain initially tried to prevent the Gulf shaikhs from signing concession agreements with non-British companies, but eventually American firms won concessions in Bahrain, Kuwait and Saudi Arabia.

The most famous petroleum partnership was the Arabian American Oil Company, known as Aramco, which was granted a concession by King Ibn Sa'ud in 1933. "If the first pillar of the Saudi state has been the Wahhabi religious movement," writes historian J.B. Kelly, "the second has been the Arabian American Oil Company.... The company has served the house of Saud as guide, confidant, tutor, counsellor, emissary, advocate, steward and factotum." Aramco promoted the image of a model company, not only seeing to the training, health care and housing of its workers, but also building roads, hospitals and water pipelines for the surrounding community. Its expatriate workers were housed in enclaves that resembled suburban America. (This benevolent image has now been challenged in a new book, *America's Kingdom: Mythmaking on the Saudi Oil Frontier*, by Robert Vitalis of the University of Pennsylvania.)

After World War II, major changes took place in the oil industry. Iran had long complained that Britain was too stingy in the compensation it paid: in 1950, the oil company forked over £16 million in royalties, whereas the company itself made £100 million in profits from its Iranian operations. When in 1950 Aramco agreed to share profits 50–50, Iran wanted to be put on the same footing as Saudi Arabia. The (now renamed) Anglo-Iranian Oil Company, however, would not agree to profit sharing. Matters came to a head when Iran's Parliament nationalized the company and Mohammad Mossadeq assumed the position of prime minister (1951–53). For Britain, this was a great humiliation and meant the loss of a key economic asset. Mossadeq's government was overthrown in August 1953 and the shah, Mohammad Reza Pahlavi, restored to power in a countercoup masterminded by U.S. and British intelligence.

Thereafter, although Iran retained sovereignty, a new agreement was struck with a consortium of oil companies to operate the concession, which reduced the British share to 40% and gave American companies an equal stake. (It was not until 1973 that Iran took full control of its oil operations.) A major consequence of the Iranian crisis was that the companies stepped up production across the Gulf, especially in Kuwait and Saudi Arabia. Commercial quantities of oil were discovered in Qatar and Abu Dhabi in 1960; in Oman in 1963; and in Dubai in 1966.

The impact of oil

The development of the oil industry set in motion many changes. In the interwar period, it began to open up the Gulf to the outside world at the expense of British control. (The British refused the U.S. permission to open any consulates in the area until 1950, when the first one opened in Kuwait.) For the first time, local rulers struck commercial deals with oil companies and now had a secure source of income independent of any British subsidy.

The Gulf area was also becoming more important as an international communication and transportation hub, with British airlines securing landing rights to stop over on the way to India. Traditional ties with the subcontinent, however, were becoming less important than relations with the greater Arab world.

With increased oil exploration came more pressure to delineate boundaries. This led, after World War II, to the protracted Buraimi oasis dispute between Saudi Arabia (backed by the U.S.) and Oman and Abu Dhabi (backed by Britain) over boundaries in the southeastern part of the peninsula, which was believed to contain oil. In 1952 Saudi troops occupied part of the oasis; arbitration failed and in 1955 they were evicted by forces from Abu Dhabi and Oman under British command.

Oil proved to be a mixed blessing. It provided salvation to Bahrain in the 1930s, when the economy collapsed along with the pearl industry. In the postwar period it funded the rapid modernization of Iran, Iraq and the Arab monarchies, some of which enjoyed a per capita income among the highest in the world. In the 1960s and 1970s, the Arab Gulf states began providing free education, health care and housing. The state also became the main employer, and, as elsewhere in the Middle East, began to exercise much closer control over its citizens. But there was also a downside: Economists have realized that natural wealth can be a curse, as natural resource exports often retard the development of industry and manufacturing for export. Even the shah of Iran, in a 1973 interview with the Italian journalist Oriana Fallaci, was ambivalent about Iran's great resource: "So much has been written about the curse we call oil, and believe me, when you have it, on the one hand it's a blessing but on the other it's a great inconvenience. Because it represents such a danger. The world could blow up on account of this damned oil."

The modernization process, which lasted for centuries in the West, has been compressed into decades in the Gulf states, putting

ROBIN LAURANCE/IMPACTPHOTOS/IMAGESTATE

A Toyota pickup truck is loaded with camels, often called the ships of the desert, in the United Arab Emirates.

great stress on traditional societies. Twentieth-century Saudi Arabian novelist Abdelrahman Munif, in the first volume of a monumental trilogy in Arabic entitled *Cities of Salt*, sensitively describes a Bedouin village's tragic encounter with American oil prospectors. The author's theme is that the discovery of oil was not a blessing but a curse, in which the desire for material gain replaced old values of loyalty, honor and respect for tradition. "The tragedy is not in our having the oil," he said in an interview, "but in the way we use the wealth it has created and in the future awaiting us after it has run out." The availability of huge oil revenues, he believes, corrupted political leaders and turned Saudi Arabia into a repressive state.

Legitimacy to rule

Although Iran and Oman have long histories as distinct territorial units, governments of the states created in the Gulf in the 20th century—Iraq, Saudi Arabia, Kuwait, Bahrain, Qatar and the UAE—keenly feel the need to create a sense of national identity. In the Arabian peninsula, governments have tried to create a historical memory and national symbols to elicit loyalty and reinforce the legitimacy of the rulers. Governments have given priority to emphasizing the cultural heritage *(turath)* of their people by carrying out archaeological excavations and building new museums and heritage villages in places such as Doha and Dubai. In the process they have emphasized their Arab, Bedouin heritage at the expense of the other groups—such as Africans, Indians, Baluch, Persians and the Hawala Arabs (those who emigrated to the Iranian side of the Gulf and later returned)—who played important roles in the cosmopolitan society that characterized the Gulf before oil. The challenge in all the Gulf states has been to reconcile traditional forms of rule with modern forms of political expression, including meaningful elections.

On the Arabian side of the Gulf, Islam and tribalism have traditionally provided legitimacy to the ruling families. In Saudi Arabia, the strict Wahhabi version of Islam has given the Al Sa'ud rulers a legitimacy that other Gulf rulers lack. However, Islam and tribalism, which previously acted as a check on the rulers, now have been adapted to serve them, points out political scientist F. Gregory Gause III. The rulers have made the clerical establishment dependent upon the state by financing the clergy, something that never happened in Shi'i Iran. The tribes are now under effective state control, although the ruler makes a public display of his fidelity to tribal institutions, such as the majlis and shura. "What most Westerners see as a 'traditional' political culture is in fact a construction of recent decades, in which rulers employ a political language redolent of Islamic and tribal overtones to convince their citizens of the legitimacy of their political system," according to Gause.

≳ ◦ ≲

Over the past century, the traditional way of life in the Arab Gulf states has been irrevocably changed, due in large measure to the British intervention and the rise of the oil industry. External and internal forces both played a role, and served to reinforce the power and wealth of one segment of their population, the ruling shaikhs. Because of the way in which the modern states were formed and boundaries arbitrarily delimited, in many cases tribal and family loyalties, and religious, linguistic and ethnic identities are more important than state citizenship. These are at the root of many present-day tensions in the region.

2

The Gulf Wars

THE PERSIAN GULF states have been profoundly transformed by three major conflicts: the Iran-Iraq War (1980–88), the Gulf War (1990–91), and the Iraq War that began in 2003. The first two wars were immensely destructive in terms of lives and infrastructure, and they inflamed sectarian tensions and raised the level of distrust among people in the littoral states. The first war carried an undertone of ethnic (Arab versus Persian) and religious (Sunni versus Shi'i) hostility, whereas the second pitted Arab against Arab, giving the lie to decades of rhetoric about pan-Arab solidarity. The last war, which ended the reign of Saddam and his Ba'ath party, was followed by U.S. occupation, prolonged instability and uncertain steps toward a new political order.

These wars focused international attention on the Gulf and, starting in 1987, prompted the U.S. to employ an unprecedented level of military might in the region. The U.S. has become the dominant power in the Gulf and has sought to protect the monarchies of the Arabian peninsula by containing first Iraqi and then Iranian influence.

The Iran-Iraq War

The single most important factor precipitating this conflict was the Iranian revolution of 1978–79, led by Ayatollah Ruhollah Khomeini. The upheaval in Iran posed a threat to Iraq, whose government was apprehensive that Khomeini's propaganda would foment unrest among Iraqi Shi'is. At the same time it presented an opportunity: Saddam hoped to overthrow the new regime, prevent the export of the revolution and possibly even annex Khuzistan, Iran's oil-rich southwestern province. Most importantly, Iraq hoped that by defeating and crippling Iran, it would gain hegemony in the Gulf.

War with Iran was a calculated risk. But Iraq believed that due to the disorganized state of the Iranian military, any defense would quickly crumble. In the summer and fall of 1980 the Iranian regime was preoccupied with fighting its internal enemies. In addition, the superpowers were unlikely to intervene: the U.S. was trying to arrange the release of its hostages, seized in the U.S. embassy in Tehran on November 4, 1979, and the U.S.S.R. was Iraq's ally.

The stated aims of the war were to obtain Iran's recognition of Iraqi sovereignty over the entire Shatt al-Arab, for Iran to desist from interfering in Iraq's internal affairs and to return the islands of Abu Musa and the Tunbs to the UAE. This last gesture was designed to demonstrate Iraq's role as the protector of the Gulf.

On September 22, 1980, Iraq bombed Tehran and invaded Khuzistan. Saddam's expectation of an easy victory was soon dashed. Iraqi forces advanced 50 miles but captured only one major city, the port of Khorramshahr. The military initiative then passed to Iran, which, in May 1992, liberated Khorramshahr and drove Iraqi troops out of Khuzistan. At this point, Iraq announced its willingness to accept binding arbitration to settle the conflict.

Iran refused. Many Iranians, who referred to the conflict as the "imposed war," were convinced that Iraq attacked Iran under orders from the U.S. and with the complicity of the U.S.S.R. in order to cause the downfall of the revolutionary government. Before Iran would agree to end the war, it stipulated that Saddam had to step down, Iraq had to be branded the aggressor by an international tribunal, and Iran had to be guaranteed large reparations. Iraq would also have to take back thousands of ethnic Persians whom it had expelled on security grounds prior to the war. From the outset, intense personal hostility between Ayatollah Khomeini and Saddam overshadowed the war.

In addition to ethnic and religious differences, Iran and Iraq also had conflicting ideologies—pan-Arabism in the case of Iraq, pan-Islam in the case of Iran. Iraq, governed by a Sunni Arab minority, stressed its ties with other Arab countries and claimed to be guarding the eastern flank of the Arab world against the spread of radical

ED KASHI/NATIONAL GEOGRAPHIC/GETTY IMAGES

Statues along the bank of the Shatt al-Arab in Basra, Iraq, point accusingly to nearby Iran in memory of Iraqis killed in the Iran-Iraq War.

Shi'ism. Khomeini, on the other hand, believed that Islamic solidarity was more important than nationalism, and that Islamic unity took precedence over present-day political frontiers.

Strategies of war

Iran launched a series of annual offensives from 1983 to 1987 to bring down Saddam's government and liberate pockets of Iranian territory held by Iraq. Iraq's strategy was to squeeze Iran economically and force it to the bargaining table. (Iran was almost wholly dependent on its oil exports through the Gulf for income, whereas Iraq exported most of its own oil via pipeline to the Mediterranean and Red seas.) Iraq destroyed Iran's refinery at Abadan and repeatedly bombed Iran's main oil-export terminal at Kharg Island in the northern Gulf. It attacked shipping bound for Iran, which responded in kind, and during the "tanker war" that ensued, the two countries attacked 543 ships, mostly from neutral nations.

Iran also sought to undermine its neighbor's economy. It formed an alliance with Syria, an Arab state governed by a rival branch of the Ba'ath party. Iran's strategy was to keep on the offensive, forcing Iraq to keep its troops in a state of readiness along a long frontier, and to refuse to negotiate despite military setbacks. The only Iranian victories were the capture of two small but strategically valuable areas, the Majnoon oil fields in February 1984 and the Fao peninsula, south of Basra, in February 1986. But Iran did not have the logistic capacity or adequate weapons to sustain its offensives for long. Although the fighting continued, Iran's leaders were divided over the wisdom of pursuing a war Tehran could not win and certainly could not afford.

Growing internationalization

The major regional response to the war was the formation in May 1981 of the GCC, which aimed to promote military and political cooperation but could do little against its two overbearing neighbors. The Gulf monarchs feared from the start that the war could spread, threatening their oil revenues and possibly their governments. They were troubled by Iraq's intentions, yet felt that they had no choice but to support it financially. The GCC states contributed an estimated $35 billion in economic and military "loans" to Iraq with little prospect they would be repaid.

Iranian leaders made it clear that their revolution was suitable for export. Some of Iran's Arab neighbors suspected Iran of sabotage and terrorism: they accused it of backing groups that attempted a coup d'état in Bahrain in December 1981 and set off explosions at the American and French embassies in Kuwait in December 1983. In early 1984, Iran warned that if it was prevented from exporting its oil, it would retaliate by closing the Strait of Hormuz. This threat greatly alarmed the West, and President Ronald Reagan (1981-89) vowed to keep the strait open. (Actually, it was too wide and deep to block physically, but the U.S. stood ready to remove any mines Iran tried to lay.)

The U.S. stake

The official U.S. policy regarding the war did not waver under the Carter (1977–81) and Reagan Administrations. The U.S. declared itself neutral; it supported the territorial integrity and political independence of both countries; it supported mediation efforts; and said it would not sell weapons to either side. In fact, however, U.S. policy increasingly tilted toward Iraq.

It was later revealed that the U.S. had actually provided aid to both sides while publicly leading a global campaign, Operation Staunch, to ban arms sales to Iran and force it to the negotiating table. The Reagan Administration secretly sold arms to Tehran in hopes of persuading Iran to order the release of American hostages held in Lebanon, and to prevent the U.S.S.R. from gaining influence in Iran. Funds from the arms sales were used to covertly support the Nicaraguan counter-revolutionaries, or *contras*. When the arms-for-hostages deal was revealed in November 1986, the resulting scandal was widely viewed as a foreign policy disaster for the Administration.

The war's end was hastened when the U.S. and others concluded by 1987 that it was too dangerous to be allowed to continue. Attacks on international shipping had increased, and Iran had sown deadly mines in the Gulf and was threatening to hit ships with Silkworm missiles. A strike by Iraqi aircraft on the USS *Stark* in May 1987 killed 37 American sailors. In order to persuade the Arab states in the Gulf of U.S. hostility toward Iran in the wake of the Iran-Contra affair and to forestall Soviet offers of help, the U.S., at the request of Kuwait, sent an armada to the Gulf in July 1987. Their mission was to assure freedom of navigation and escort Kuwaiti oil tankers, which had been "reflagged," or transferred to U.S. registry.

The U.S. now turned to the UN in search of a solution. On July 20, 1987, the Security Council passed Resolution 598, which demanded a cease-fire, the withdrawal of forces to international boundaries, an exchange of prisoners, formal negotiations for a permanent settlement and the establishment of a tribunal to judge responsibility for the war. The resolution tilted in favor of Iraq, which promptly accepted it, but to the surprise of many, Iran did not reject it.

In early 1988, Iraq stepped up military pressure on Iran. In March, Baghdad unleashed an estimated 150 Soviet-made missiles against Tehran, terrifying the population. It also used chemical weapons, which demoralized Iranian troops. A string of Iraqi victories on land, including the recapture of Fao, revealed Iran's weakness. The U.S. seized and blew up an Iranian vessel it caught red-handed laying mines in September 1987 and destroyed Iranian oil platforms in October 1987 and April 1988. Such actions helped persuade the Iranians that they could not win. The last straw was when the USS *Vincennes,* fearing it was about to be attacked, mistakenly downed an Iranian civilian airliner in July, killing 290 aboard. To the surprise of all, Ayatollah Khomeini decided to "swallow poison," accept Resolution 598, and end the war. A cease-fire has been in effect since August 20, 1988.

Aftermath and lessons

The Iran-Iraq War was the longest and one of the costliest conventional wars of this century. Casualties are estimated at over a million, with approximately 400,000 killed and 700,000 injured, on both sides. When the war ended, neither side had achieved its aims and each felt that outside powers had cheated it out of victory. *The Economist* (London) commented, "This was a war that should never have been fought.... neither side gained a thing, except the saving of its own regime. And neither regime was worth the sacrifice."

In Iran, and especially Iraq, the conflict itself and the demonization of the opponent led to a stronger sense of national identity. Iran's calculation that the Shi'i majority in southern Iraq would rally to its cause, and Iraq's reckoning that the Arab citizens in Khuzistan would welcome the Iraqi army as their liberators, were both wrong. The war helped the revolutionary government in Tehran consolidate power and distracted attention from pressing economic and social problems. Indeed, it was not until the leadership feared the revolution itself was in danger that they agreed to the cease-fire proposal.

The main reason for Western involvement in the war was to protect oil exports. Paradoxically, although there were short-term fluctuations, the price of oil did not go up but remained depressed, despite the war on shipping in the Gulf.

The Iran-Iraq War was an anomaly for the Middle East because it was the first time in which the superpowers had ended up on the same side. This partly resulted from the U.S.S.R.'s preoccupation with its own internal problems. Although both professed neutrality, both in fact aided Iraq—the U.S.S.R. with arms, and the U.S. with economic, diplomatic and intelligence support—despite the fact that Iran was acknowledged to be the greater prize strategically. The superpowers' cooperation paved the way for greater unity during the Gulf War. The war also demonstrated the importance of the UN in conflict resolution, which would be a key factor in the Gulf War.

From war to war

The failure of Iraq to prevail in its war with Iran led directly to its invasion of Kuwait two years later. This momentous event, on August 2, 1990, altered political alignments in the Middle East, imperiled world energy supplies and confronted the U.S. and the U.S.S.R. with the first international crisis since the end of the cold war. It also marked the resumption of Saddam's quest to dominate the Gulf.

The Iraqi leader evidently regarded the capture of Kuwait as a low-risk adventure that its Arab neighbors would be powerless to reverse. Iraq's active armed forces totaled 1 million, by far the largest in the region (Kuwait had an army of 20,000), were battle-tested and well-armed. Saddam calculated that his ally, the U.S.S.R., would not intervene, nor would the U.S.—which passed up an opportunity to warn him off.

"The mistake in the Arab world as well as the West was not to recognize the desperation of Saddam's situation," according to scholars Lawrence Freedman and Efraim Karsh. There were several reasons for the attack. One was financial. Iran ended the war with virtually no foreign debt, whereas Iraq was left with a debt estimated as high as $80 billion, about half of which was owed to Saudi Arabia, Kuwait and the UAE. Although the Saudis did not press for reimbursement, Kuwait showed no readiness to forgive or reduce the debt. Kuwait and the UAE also deliberately overproduced in violation of Organization of Petroleum Exporting Countries (OPEC) production quotas, which depressed the price and hurt Iraq. In addition, Iraq charged that Kuwait was unfairly drawing oil from the giant Rumaila field, which straddled their common border. In February and July 1990, Saddam demanded more money from the Gulf states but they turned him down.

Saddam also needed to keep his huge army occupied, and Iraqis would likely be sympathetic to annexing Kuwait. In a way, Kuwait would be a consolation prize since he had failed to wrest Khuzistan from Iran. Annexing Kuwait would solve Iraq's financial problems and give Iraq a fine harbor on the Gulf. It would also lessen tension with Iran since it would greatly reduce the significance of who controlled the Shatt al-Arab.

The Western powers responded promptly to the invasion of Kuwait. President George H.W. Bush (1989–93) declared that "the acquisition of territory by force is unacceptable" and demanded Iraq's "unconditional and complete withdrawal." In announcing the dispatch of U.S. forces to Saudi Arabia in Operation Desert Shield on August 8, 1990, Bush declared that "a line has been drawn in the sand" to forestall an Iraqi invasion of Saudi Arabia. Economic sanctions and a naval embargo were placed on Iraq, and throughout the fall Americans—and others—debated whether they would work.

Iraqi President Saddam Hussein waves to supporters in Baghdad, Iraq, on October 18, 1995, one day after being sworn in as president for another seven years.

By its forceful response to the crisis, the U.S. demonstrated that the "Vietnam syndrome"—the aversion to foreign involvement that gripped Americans in the wake of the Vietnam War—was over. In explaining his decision to send troops, President Bush said that the independence of Saudi Arabia was "of vital interest" to the U.S. He insisted that if Saddam got away with annexing Kuwait, world order would be endangered.

There was widespread confusion, however, over U.S. objectives. In November Bush declared, "The fight isn't about oil. The fight is about naked aggression that will not stand." Bush compared Saddam to Adolf Hitler and emphasized the dangers of appeasement. But later, Secretary of State James A. Baker III, emphasizing the war's economic consequences, said the main reason the U.S. was in Saudi Arabia was to protect American jobs.

Bush sought above all to make it clear that Iraq, by its act of ag-

37

gression, stood condemned not by the U.S. alone but by the world. In this he was largely successful. He mobilized an international coalition against Iraq and initiated a series of resolutions in the UN Security Council, including one calling for an embargo on trade with Iraq and another that authorized the use of force if Iraq did not withdraw from Kuwait by January 15, 1991. By that time, there were 560,000 U.S. troops in the Gulf in preparation for a ground war.

One of the most striking aspects of the crisis was the unprecedented degree of superpower cooperation. In truth, at the time, the U.S.S.R. was not in a position to oppose the U.S. The very survival of the Soviet state was in question as communism crumbled in Eastern Europe and Moscow moved toward a more-open political system and market-oriented economy. It was badly in need of U.S. aid for reconstruction.

The regional response

The crisis in the Gulf took Middle Easterners by surprise; the Kuwaiti royalty barely had time to escape. By inviting American troops to defend the kingdom, the House of Sa'ud risked condemnation by fellow Arabs (and Saudis themselves) for giving outside powers, and non-Muslims at that, a chance to gain a foothold in the region. Partly thanks to the persuasive powers of Egypt's President Mubarak, a majority of the Arab League, which at the time represented 20 Arab nations and the Palestine Liberation Organization (PLO), approved a resolution sending Arab forces to join U.S., British and French troops in Saudi Arabia.

Although it did not take part in the Gulf War, Iran was a beneficiary. At the outset of the war, in order to neutralize Iran, Saddam did a major about-face and appeared to accept the Iranian position on sharing the Shatt al-Arab. During the war, Iran condemned the presence of U.S. forces in the Gulf, but it also called for the restoration of the ruling family in Kuwait. By not opposing the alliance against Iraq, Iran earned a measure of gratitude from the West and had the satisfaction of seeing the military potential of its former enemy severely curtailed. It is especially significant that Iran refrained from giving much assistance to the postwar Shi'i revolt in southern Iraq.

The 'mother of all battles'

After a tortured national debate that lasted throughout the fall of 1990, Congress voted on January 12, 1991, to authorize the use of force to remove the Iraqi army from Kuwait, if it did not comply with a UN Security Council resolution and withdraw within three days. Saddam ignored the deadline, and allied air strikes began on January 16. Iraq's response was indecisive, with no major attack on the allied forces, only desultory SCUD missile attacks on Saudi Arabia, Bahrain and Israel. Following over a month of bombing, which pulverized Iraq's infrastructure, an allied ground assault, "Desert Storm," began on February 23. In 100 hours, Kuwait was recaptured from the Iraqi army.

The question of why the U.S. abruptly halted the hostilities and did not pursue Saddam and his forces has haunted those who fought the war. At the time, the Administration was concerned that if it marched on Baghdad and replaced the government, it would lose the support of its Arab allies and find itself in a quagmire. It was not willing to assume responsibility for administering Iraq and had no UN mandate to do so. The U.S. also did not want to destabilize Iraq, which was and is the only Gulf state that can check the power of Iran. In retrospect, many believe that the U.S. stopped the war too soon. At the time that General Norman Schwarzkopf, the allied commander, declared in Riyadh, Saudi Arabia, that "the gate is closed" and Iraqi troops were trapped, in reality two thirds of the elite Republican Guard were escaping. Continuing the war for another day or two could have assured the Iraqi special forces' destruction.

American casualties were miraculously few: only 148 Americans were killed in action (including 35 by "friendly fire") and 467 wounded. However, a major report, "Gulf War Illness and the Health of Gulf War Veterans," mandated by Congress and issued in November 2008, concluded that persistent health problems, often dubbed Gulf War Syndrome, affected about one in four U.S. veterans of the Gulf War (upward of 175,000 people). The primary cause appears to be pills taken to neutralize nerve gas, as well as exposure to insecticides. In contrast to a 1996 report that blamed Gulf War Syndrome on wartime stress or psychiatric illness, the more recent report concluded that "scientific evidence leaves no question that Gulf War illness is a real condition with real causes and serious consequences for affected veterans."

Aftermath

Despite the swift triumph on the battlefield and the restoration of Kuwaiti sovereignty, many feared that the U.S. had won the war and lost the peace. Although President Bush believed he would be overthrown, Saddam remained in power and he lost no time in crushing rebellions by Shi'i Arabs in the south and Kurds in the north that the U.S. had encouraged. President Bush later acknowledged that mistakes had been made at the armistice meeting at Safwan, Iraq, after the war. At that time, General Schwarzkopf gave Iraq permission to fly armed helicopters anywhere inside the country, as long as they were away from American forces. This enabled Saddam to crush the uprisings.

For the Iraqi people, the results of the war were devastating. Initial estimates of 100,000 soldiers killed and 300,000 wounded, however, were wildly inflated. The true total will never be known, but is probably around 20,000 dead and 60,000 wounded, according to both Iraqi estimates and the U.S. Central Command.

There is no doubting the physical destruction. A UN team that visited in March 1991 found that the bombardment had "wrought near apocalyptic results upon the infrastructure....Iraq has...been relegated to a preindustrial age, but with all the postindustrial dependency on an intensive use of energy and technology." Five years after the war, water and sewage systems were still in ruins, food production had fallen 30%, and 4,500 children were dying each month because of hunger or disease, according to the UN Children's Fund. Before the sanctions were imposed, Iraq had imported about $360 million worth of drugs a year, a figure that in 1996 had dropped to about $33 million. Iraq also experienced a serious brain drain due to the emigration of its foreign-educated elite.

Sanctions and inspections

After the end of the Gulf War, the coalition forces imposed stringent conditions on Iraq that seriously restricted its sovereignty. Under UN Resolution 687 of April 1991, Iraq was required to disclose the extent of its programs to develop chemical, nuclear and biological weapons and ballistic missiles, and to dismantle them. Iraq also had to agree to long-term UN monitoring to verify it was not rearming. Only after this was done could sanctions be lifted. A UN Special Commission for the Disarmament of Iraq (Unscom), which operated from 1991 until December 1998, monitored compliance. Unscom inspectors, while engaged in a cat-and-mouse game with Baghdad, discovered that Iraq had been conducting a clandestine nuclear program that, had it continued, might have led to a weapon by late 1992. Significantly, it did not find any nuclear stockpiles, although questions remained about chemical and biological weapons. Unscom inspectors were pulled out in November 1998 in advance of a major allied bombing campaign (Operation Desert Fox) against presumed weapons sites in mid-December. A new body, the United Nations Monitoring, Verification and Inspection Commission (Unmovic) later operated in Iraq from November 2002 until the outbreak of hostilities in March 2003. The head of Unmovic, Hans Blix, reported to the Security Council on March 7 that "no evidence of proscribed activities have so far been found." By then the second Bush Administration, convinced that Iraq possessed WMDs, was on a fast track to war.

To alleviate the dire humanitarian conditions inside Iraq, the UN approved an "oil-for-food" program that took effect in December 1996. This allowed limited oil sales and was the first significant infusion of funds to Iraq in six years. The UN closely supervised the disbursement of funds, with money going to buy food and medicines, pay for war reparations, and to reimburse the UN for its monitoring operation. The program was subsequently expanded and limits were removed on the amount of oil that could be sold. By 2001, sanctions were becoming less effective due to "sanctions fatigue" and lack of support by neighboring countries, which were appalled by the suffering of the Iraqi people. Also, the illegal smuggling of oil by the regime was providing a good income.

The internal revolts

Following Baghdad's brutal suppression of the internal revolts by Shi'is and Kurds after the war, the UN Security Council adopted Resolution 688, which demanded that the Iraqi government stop suppressing its own citizens, especially in the Kurdish areas. The allied powers and neighboring states agreed that they would not recognize an independent Kurdish state. But the U.S., in cooperation with Turkey, Britain and France, started Operation Provide Comfort. To provide a safe haven for the Kurds, Iraqi forces were forbidden from flying fixed-wing aircraft above the 36th parallel. On January 1, 1997, with the withdrawal of the French from air patrols, the operation was renamed Northern Watch. This continued until March 17, 2003, the eve of the coalition attack.

In August 1992, the U.S. and its allies in the Gulf War also banned flights by Iraqi aircraft south of the 32nd parallel; in September 1996, this was extended to the 33rd parallel. This protection was originally provided after the U.S. realized that the Shi'is were not about to ally with Iran but might help bring about Saddam's downfall. The objective was also to prevent Iraqi forces from massing for an attack on Kuwait or Saudi Arabia. Air cover, however, did not prevent Saddam from moving tanks and artillery into the region and decimating any opposition. In addition to military pressure, Saddam adopted a simpler expedient to crush the Marsh Arabs, or Madan, in the south, who were being punished for sympathizing with and aiding Shi'i rebels. He drained their marshes, denying them refuge, and in the process almost destroyed their unique culture.

Iraq and the Gulf states

Under the terms of the UN cease-fire resolution, a commission was formed to determine the *de jure* border between Iraq and Kuwait, which it did in April 1992. The new official border benefited Kuwait by granting it a large part of the Rumaila oil field and the southern part of Iraq's port of Umm Qasr. These boundary revisions angered Iraq, although it formally accepted them in November 1994.

One goal of the war with Iran, and later of the annexation of Kuwait, was to enhance Iraq's access to the Gulf and recognition as a Gulf power. After the Gulf War, "Baghdad's actions were based on the regime's stubborn refusal to submit to the role of the vanquished and to accept the full consequences of the invasion of Kuwait and its aftermath," according to Raad Alkadiri, an analyst at PFC Energy in Washington. Iraq sought to break out of its isolation and avoid the sanctions by cultivating ties to other Arab states, particularly those in the GCC. (Kuwait and Saudi Arabia were supportive of U.S. policy and favored continued containment.) By the fall of 2000 Iraq had again become a player in regional politics. However, under the leadership of Saddam, Iraq remained a stalled society and it appeared would remain so until he left office. With the advent of the new Administration of George W. Bush in January 2001, U.S. patience wore out and a war of choice was waged to replace Saddam and remake Iraq.

Operation Iraqi Freedom

The policies of Bush II (2001–2009) were shaped by the attacks on the World Trade Center and the Pentagon on September 11, 2001. The following month he initiated a war that ousted the Taliban from Afghanistan, although he was unsuccessful in apprehending bin Laden, the leader of al-Qaeda headquartered there. He was convinced that Saddam was implicated in the attacks, and his Administration often maintained there was a link between al-Qaeda and Iraq. Bush signaled his intentions in his State of the Union speech in January 2002, which designated Iraq (along with Iran and North Korea) as part of an "axis of evil" that threatened the peace of the world. He announced that the U.S. war on terror had just begun, and that the U.S. "will not permit the world's most dangerous regimes to threaten us with the world's most destructive weapons." Over the following year, his Administration made the case for putting an end to the regime of Saddam. A congressional resolution authorizing the use of U.S. forces against Iraq passed easily and was signed into law on October 16, 2002.

In contrast to the war waged by his father, Bush II did not have the support of the UN, major U.S. allies (with the exception of Britain, Italy and Spain) or most of the international community.

The case for preemptive military action was based on the belief that Iraq possessed WMDs and might transfer them to terrorist groups such as al-Qaeda. A subsequent rationale was that remaking Iraq as a democracy would lead to a wave of similar regimes in the Middle East. Skeptics believed that the U.S. wanted to control Iraqi oil and that the Bush Administration had calculated that the oil revenues would pay for the war. All of these notions were later disproved. In a televised ultimatum on March 17, 2003, Bush gave Saddam and his sons 48 hours to leave Iraq or he (Bush) warned military conflict would ensue, telling the Iraqi people "the day of your liberation is near."

The U.S. campaign began prematurely on March 20, with an attack on a location in Baghdad where Saddam and his top leadership were mistakenly believed to be gathered. The main "shock and awe" bombardment began on March 21, followed by an invasion of U.S. and British troops, who pushed rapidly inland in a rush to take Baghdad. (Although the forces were referred to as an international "coalition of the willing," other nations did not send combat troops.) There were fewer casualties than expected, little damage to historical and religious sites and infrastructure such as bridges was left mostly intact.

The Baghdad airport was taken on April 3, and on April 9 iconic images were broadcast to the world of rapturous Iraqis tearing down a statue of Saddam. Defying expectations, U.S. tanks met little resistance in Baghdad and Ba'ath officials had largely escaped before the coalition forces arrived. Many suspected a deal that had spared American, British and Iraqi lives, averted a bloodbath, and accelerated the end of the war. The fall of Tikrit, Saddam's hometown, on April 14 marked the end of major combat. Bush's speech on an aircraft carrier off the California coast on May 1, with a large banner proclaiming "Mission Accomplished" as a backdrop, was the highwater mark of victory. After that, everything seemed to go wrong.

Although the U.S. developed a successful war plan that rapidly defeated the Iraqi army, it quickly became clear that little thought had gone into consolidating the victory and dealing with postwar Iraq. This was partly due to bureaucratic infighting in Washington

U.S. Marines helped topple the iconic statue of Saddam Hussein in central Baghdad on April 9, 2003. This image became an enduring symbol of his ouster.

among the Pentagon, State Department, White House and intelligence agencies. "...It is difficult to overstate what a key misstep this lack of strategic direction was—probably the single most significant miscalculation of the entire effort," according to Thomas E. Ricks, a *Washington Post* correspondent who covered the conflict. The small number of troops committed to the battle, at the direction of Defense Secretary Donald Rumsfeld, was widely criticized and became a serious concern once victory had been secured. Some in the Bush Administration had believed promises by Iraqi emigrés like Ahmad Chalabi (favored by the Pentagon) that the Americans would be greeted as liberators and would face little resistance. Unfortunately, this did not prove to be the case.

In the aftermath of the fall of the Saddam regime, there was widespread lawlessness throughout the country that the small number of coalition troops could not quell. In the race to Baghdad, for example, many towns in southern Iraq that harbored regime loyalists had been bypassed. In the capital itself, there was widespread looting and destruction (dismissed by Rumsfeld as "stuff happens"). Iraqis were impatient for humanitarian relief to reach them and for reconstruction to begin.

Postwar politics

The chaos and confusion of postwar politics in Iraq began immediately and continues to this day. The problem that doomed the British mission in Iraq after World War I and was carefully avoided by Bush I after the first Gulf War—administering an occupied country—now confronted the U.S. The first official charged with organizing reconstruction and relief efforts was retired Army General Jay Garner, who lasted only three weeks on the job in Baghdad. He was replaced by Ambassador L. Paul Bremer III, who was regarded as a U.S. proconsul and took actions that significantly affected the future of Iraq. He led the Coalition Provisional Authority (CPA), which disbanded the army, throwing 450,000 Iraqi military men out of work, and implemented an extensive de-Ba'athification campaign. (These actions ignored the fact that to hold any high-level position in Iraq one had to be a member of the Ba'ath, and membership did not necessarily imply support for government policies.) The dismissal of the troops led to desperation and some took up armed struggle against the occupiers. Bremer also appointed the Governing Council of Iraqis, which was divided among the sectarian groups, with a majority of seats going to the Shi'i. The CPA was widely regarded as out of touch and unable to provide security for Iraqis, and by the winter of 2003–2004 many Iraqis had turned against the occupation and the insurgency expanded. (Saddam was captured in December 2003; brought to trial in October 2005; and executed in December 2006.) In June 2004 the CPA transferred authority to a new interim government headed by Ayad Allawi that set the stage for elections in January 2005. Iraq, once again, would be ruled by Iraqis.

3

The Future of Iraq

THE TRAGEDY OF IRAQ is the disparity between the key role the country has played in the history of civilization and Islamic society and the difficult circumstances in which it finds itself in the early 21st century. Iraq has many things going for it, including a favorable geographical situation with two great rivers (the Tigris and Euphrates), fertile soil, a relatively large population, and rich natural resources, including the world's third-largest oil reserves. But the fulfillment of its great potential has repeatedly been thwarted.

Historically, the area that comprises present-day Iraq was known as Mesopotamia, the land between the rivers. It was host to the Sumerian, Babylonian and Assyrian empires. This land, indeed, was the crucible of civilization where Ur, the traditional birthplace of Abraham, was located. It is here that writing, the wheel and the 60-minute hour were invented. In the 7th century A.D., Arab invaders from the south claimed it for Islam. From the 8th to the 13th centuries Baghdad was the capital of the Abbasid Caliphate, widely regarded as the "Golden Age of Islam." The historical development of Iran and Iraq was closely intertwined until the Mongol invasions of the 13th century. After that, Iraq declined in importance, and the Middle East was increasingly split into an Arab zone centered in Egypt, and Persian and Turkish zones.

The territory that became Iraq was governed by the Ottoman Empire, based in Istanbul, for 400 years starting in the mid-16th century. During that time, it consisted of three provinces: Mosul in the north, Baghdad in the center and Basra in the south. After World War I, Britain united the provinces to form the new country. Iraq's myriad communities, however, had little sense of national identity.

Iraq was a British mandate from 1920 until it became independent in 1932. Under the Hashemite monarchy (1921–58) the British enjoyed military privileges there and the country's foreign policy was pro-Western. In 1955 Iraq signed a mutual defense treaty with Britain, Iran, Pakistan and Turkey called the Baghdad Pact; after Iraq dropped out in 1959, it was renamed the Central Treaty Organization. From the beginning, the army has played a disproportionate role in the state and initiated a number of military coups, starting in 1936. The army's crushing of a revolt by Assyrians (Nestorian Christians) in 1933 was an ominous precedent for later military interventions in internal affairs.

The monarchy was overthrown in 1958 and replaced by a strongly nationalistic government hostile to the West and Israel. From 1968 until 2003 Iraq was ruled by the Ba'ath party, with its leader, Saddam Hussein, at the top level of government and president since 1979. Ba'athist party ideology as originally formulated was an idealistic combination of socialism and Arab unity, but it later degenerated into an instrument to legitimate Saddam and orchestrate mass support for the regime.

For years, Iraq was ruled by a small "community of trust," made up of kinsmen who would not betray each other, according to Charles Tripp of the University of London. Saddam, of peasant background from the provincial town of Tikrit, long relied on a circle of relatives from his hometown. He fostered a political culture characterized by suspicion and violence. Iraq became a "Republic of Fear," in the words of dissident Kanan Makiya, as the regime exercised rigid control and tolerated no dissent. In ways unlike other Middle Eastern countries, the state's routine use of violence against internal threats complemented its external aggression. Iraq was a rentier state that benefited from high oil revenues in the 1970s, although during its war with Iran in the 1980s it turned to extortion from the GCC monarchies, claiming it was protecting them from Iran. Above all, the country was at the mercy of the dictator, Saddam.

State and society

As economic historian Charles Issawi reminds us, "At the beginning of this century, Iraq was, even by Middle Eastern standards, a very backward country. Egypt, Turkey, and Syria were far ahead of it in such indices of development as foreign trade, transportation, industrialization, education and availability of urban amenities. Only Iran stood at a comparable level." Considering where it started, in the early decades Iraq made considerable progress in creating a unified state, in terms of infrastructure, education and health care, as well as a Parliament, an army and a bureaucracy. In the post-World War II period a substantial urban middle class arose and Iraqis had high aspirations. Until about 1990, Iraqi governments placed a high priority on instilling a national identity, deemphasizing differences between the largest sectarian communities: Arab Shi'is, Arab Sunnis and Kurds.

Iraq today has a population of some 33 million, which is about 95% Muslim and two thirds urban. It is divided into three large communities: Shi'i Arabs are believed to constitute around 55% of the population, Sunni Arabs about 18% to 19%, and Kurds about 19% to 21%. The Sunni Arabs monopolized political power both under the Ottomans and in independent Iraq. Shi'i are concentrated in the southern half of the country from Baghdad to the Gulf and were largely excluded from power until 2003. The Kurds are a non-Arab, mostly Sunni ethnic group living predominantly in the mountainous north, who fought the central government for decades for more autonomy. After the 1990–91 Gulf War, they got it. Since 2003, they have formed a political alliance with the Shi'i and together dominate the political landscape of the state.

An undated file photo depicts Iraq's most revered Shiʻi cleric, Grand Ayatollah Ali Sistani. He is based in Najaf, Iraq, and ascended to the level of a Grand Ayatollah in 1992.

Iraq's strategic predicament

Because of their country's historical experience, Iraqis feel deeply vulnerable to outside forces that they believe constantly threaten the state. Although Iraq's orientation in the 20th century was often westward, toward the Fertile Crescent and Turkey, since the overthrow of the monarchy and the rise of Saddam it has sought to become a power in the Persian Gulf. Iraqis blame their unfavorable strategic situation on the British, who arbitrarily drew the boundaries of the new state and prevented it from gaining a secure foothold there. This has led to periodic demands by Baghdad that Kuwait be "returned" to it. When Kuwait attained independence in 1961, Iraq laid claim to it and Britain sent in troops (later replaced by those of the Arab League) to protect it. In 1963, a later government in Iraq recognized Kuwait's independence.

In order to use its major seaport, Basra, ships must pass up the Shatt al-Arab waterway, which serves as the border with Iran. This has led to long-standing demands by Iraq that it control the entire Shatt al-Arab. A 1975 treaty Iran and Iraq signed in Algiers stipulated that the boundary was to be the median line, as Iran wanted. Saddam repudiated this when he went to war with Iran in 1980, yet at the outset of the occupation of Kuwait in 1990, he appeared to agree to the Iranian position.

Iraq developed another small port, Umm Qasr, on an inlet near Kuwait, and to assure access to it has unsuccessfully demanded control over the Kuwaiti islands of Warba and Bubiyan. Under the UN determination of the maritime border in March 1993, Iraqi ships must transit Kuwaiti waters in the Khor Abdullah to reach their own port, which is a continuing source of complaint. In the summer of 2011, tensions arose after Kuwait began building the massive Mubarak port on Bubiyan island, with Iraq objecting that it would block its access to shipping lanes and "strangle" the trade of Basra. Since neither of its southern borders have been resolved to Iraq's satisfaction, they may be the focus of future conflict.

Iraq is largely dependent upon the goodwill of others to export its major resource, oil. Two terminals located offshore of Fao, at the mouth of the Shatt al-Arab, export 80% of Iraq's oil. But they were built in 1975 and are now crumbling. (In the spring of 2009, Iran asserted for the first time that these terminals were in Iranian waters.) Otherwise Iraq must rely on a pipeline via Turkey (subject to insurgent attacks and until recently closed due to pricing disputes), with pipelines via Syria and Saudi Arabia both closed. Although Iraq plans to build new infrastructure, the lack of an assured ability to export its oil has led to frustration and insecurity on the part of Iraqi leaders.

Iraq is also dependent on neighboring states for most of its water resources, above all from the Tigris and Euphrates rivers, which originate in southeastern Turkey. Major dams under construction in Turkey since the 1970s (the GAP project) and in Syria are constricting the amount of water Iraq receives. Iraqi relations with these states have sometimes been tense, and lack of adequate water could lead to conflict in the future. Iran controls the flow of the Karun River into the Shatt al-Arab and has sometimes restricted it, to the consternation of Iraqis. The shortage of water, combined with a drought and associated sandstorms over the past several years, has caused a crisis in Iraqi agriculture and public health. In addition, saltwater now has intruded into the Shatt al-Arab beyond Basra, seriously compromising the quality of drinking water and making it unsuitable for irrigation.

The political response to Iraq's strategic predicament could have been to cultivate good relations with its neighbors. But it has unfortunately done the opposite: created a series of authoritarian, military-

---

The Kurds: 'No friends but the mountains'

THE Gulf War of 1990–91 led to longed-for autonomy for Iraq's Kurds. An ancient Middle Eastern nation numbering an estimated 30 million, the Kurds are dispersed among Turkey (where they constitute around 24% of the population), Iraq (21%), Iran (11%), Syria (10%) and in the Caucasus and Central Asia. They comprise the largest ethnic group in the Middle East after the Arabs, Persians and Turks, and are one of the largest nations today with no state of their own. The majority are Sunni Muslims and speak Kurdish, an Iranian language. About half of all Kurds live in cities. Traditionally, Kurds have given their allegiance to extended families and clans, not purely political figures.

After World War I, the Kurds were one of the minorities who were not able to establish their own independent state. Original promises by the allies for Kurdish autonomy or independence contained in the Treaty of Sèvres (1920) were forgotten when modern Turkey's boundaries were recognized in the Treaty of Lausanne (1923). The rich oil resources of the province of Mosul were awarded to the new state of Iraq. The fragmented Kurdish community has pursued a struggle for greater autonomy, if not outright independence, within the various countries ever since. Kurds briefly established their own Soviet-backed republic in Mahabad, Iran, in 1945–46. Only in Iraq and Turkey, however, have they posed a continuing threat to the rule of the central government. Turkey has attempted to suppress the identity of the Kurds living within its borders and since 1984 has been locked in a bitter, on-again, off-again conflict with the PKK, which initially sought independence but has now modified its demands and seeks dominated regimes that espoused a strong Iraqi nationalism. Baghdad governments have often been often suspicious of neighboring states, and sometimes with good reason. Turkey has carried out cross-border raids in pursuit of Kurdish rebels of the Kurdistan Workers party (PKK) taking refuge in the mountains of Iraqi Kurdistan, while Iran long hosted an Iraqi Shiʻi opposition in exile. The Israeli destruction of an Iraqi nuclear reactor in 1981 was another unwelcome reminder

equal cultural and political rights for Turkey's Kurds. In August 2011, Turkey carried out hundreds of airstrikes against suspected Kurdish insurgent bases in northern Iraq.

During Iraq's war with Iran in the 1980s, Kurdish guerrillas (the Peshmerga) took control of large parts of northern Iraq. However, Iraqi forces struck back with a vengeance, gassing the small border town of Halabja

MANCA JUVAN/IN PICTURES/CORBIS

Kurds participate in the ancient Pir-i Shaliar ceremony at a shrine in the village of Uraman in Iran's Kurdistan province.

of Iraq's vulnerability. In light of these threats, many Western analysts found it easy to believe that the Iraqi military sought an "equalizer" in WMDs. This was erroneous, and in interrogations after his capture, Saddam admitted he was more afraid of Iran learning he had disarmed than of the U.S. believing he had WMDs.

Governing Iraq

"The long-term legacy of the British occupation and mandate of Iraq was a weak state buttressed by relatively strong and powerful armed forces, which took power in the late 1950s in the face of the inadequacy of the state," according to historian Peter Sluglett. "As an

---

and killing an estimated 4,000 civilians in March 1988. After the August cease-fire, they destroyed hundreds of Kurdish villages and transferred their populations to detention camps in other parts of the country.

In March 1991, after allied forces had routed the Iraqi army, a popular uprising broke out among Shi'i of southern Iraq, and it was quickly followed by one among the Kurds. Kurdish rebels seized much of northern Iraq. The U.S. did not want to see the emergence of an independent Kurdistan and did not aid the rebels. Forces loyal to Saddam brutally turned on the Kurds, causing at least 1.5 million refugees to flee to the Turkish and Iranian border areas. The U.S., along with Britain and France, and with the cooperation of Turkey, then instituted a relief effort and pledged that the Kurdish zone would remain a safe haven.

Iraqi Kurdistan became virtually independent under the protection of the U.S., and was a peaceful refuge in contrast to the rest of Iraq. (The areas controlled by Kurds included other minority groups, such as Arabs, Assyrians, Turkomans and Chaldeans.) After the fall of Saddam, a Kurdistan Regional Government (KRG) was established, which has wide legal authority, including its own constitution and Parliament and a president, Massoud Barzani. The two principal groups that make up the KRG are the Kurdistan Democratic party (KDP), led by Barzani, and the Patriotic Union of Kurdistan (PUK), led by Jalal Talabani. Barzani and Talabani are traditional leaders who are bitter rivals, although they have cooperated closely since 2003. Each represents a different subdivision of Kurds (Bar-

---

institution, the state is not deeply rooted in society, and its generally repressive nature means that it enjoys little popular support. As far as they can, its citizens turn their backs on it and try to do without it, exploiting networks of family, kin, tribe, village, ethnicity, and so on." This legacy has made it difficult to create a national political community in the wake of the U.S. occupation.

The political priority for Iraqi governments from 1920 until 1990 was to create an Iraqi national identity that would subsume differences of ethnicity, religion and tribe. An Iraqi nationalism arose that was tested and reaffirmed by the war with Iran, in which Iraqis fought for their country and were not swayed by the religious appeals of Ayatollah Kho-

---

zani is from northern Kurdistan and Talabani from central Kurdistan), and each speaks a different dialect of Kurdish. In the elections of 2010 the KDP emerged much stronger than the PUK, while a new reform party, Gorran ("Change"), took 8 of the 57 seats won by the entire Kurdish Alliance.

Since 2003, Kurds have for the first time played a prominent role in the central government, shaping legislation and achieving high office, including the Iraqi president, Talabani, and the country's foreign minister, Hoshyar Zebari. Tension continues, however, between the Arab Shi'i-dominated central government and the Kurdish regional government. Major differences still need to be resolved with Baghdad over the status of the oil-rich city of Kirkuk, which the Kurds would like to absorb into the KRG, and over oil policy, with the government contesting their right to sign contracts with foreign oil companies, and the amount of revenue that they are entitled to.

Kurdish political factions have historically been subject to manipulation by outsiders, which has hindered Kurdish unity. A power struggle between these factions, and between Kurds and the central government, seems likely to continue, with Kurds showing little willingness to compromise over issues such as Kirkuk. This is causing a major complication for the U.S. withdrawal. Although at present the Kurds are willing to settle for autonomy, future independence is still a dream for many. However, neighboring countries, as well as external powers, do not want to see the emergence of an independent Kurdistan. As the Kurds like to say, when the chips are down, they have no friends but the mountains. ✿

meini. However, in the wake of war and the violent uprisings of Kurds and Shi'i Arabs in 1991, Saddam's government, in an attempt to divide potential opposition, instituted a process of "retribalization," in which substate identities were emphasized and Sunni Arabs were firmly in control. This policy went against everything Ba'athism stood for and has contributed to the unraveling of Iraq in the post-Saddam era.

Ethnic and sectarian representation continue to be taken into account in political appointments. Thus the Iraqi Governing Council appointed by the CPA in July 2003, and the Cabinet it appointed in turn, each contained 13 Shi'i members, 5 Sunnis, 5 Kurds, and 2 from small communities such as the Turkoman and Chaldean Christians. Subsequent Iraqi Cabinets also followed such guidelines, and excluded Sunni former Ba'athists. This practice, along with the identification of political parties with ethnic or religious groups, has led some to wonder whether Iraq was a viable state or could break up. As *New York Times* reporter Anthony Shadid remarked, "No one speaks for the nation in Iraq. Perhaps there really isn't one."

The problem, according to political scientist Eric Davis, is exacerbated by the tendency of scholars and politicians to analyze Iraq in terms of its Shi'is, Sunnis and Kurds, and peoples' supposed loyalties to such groups instead of the state: "From this assumption, it is only a short conceptual leap to the theoretical conclusion that the region's political instability and violence are a function of defective political culture." Authoritarian rule then becomes the logical solution.

The possibility that Iraq would break down along ethnic and sectarian lines was feared by some in the U.S. at the time of the internal revolts in 1991. After the U.S. invasion in 2003, some kind of partition seemed a real possibility. These fears now seem overblown, although the strength of Kurdish identity in the north could eventually lead to separation. While the central government in Baghdad is weak, the integration of Iraqi society has gone too far to permit a breakup, in the opinion of Iraqi scholar Isam al-Khafaji. The artificiality of Iraq, he maintains, is a myth. Rather, he points to the forces of integration at work since the early 19th century. He interprets the loyalty of the (largely Shi'a) Iraqi army during the war with Iran and the fact that, after almost two decades of autonomy, no Kurdish state has been declared in the north, as evidence that nationalism has now taken precedence over sectarian identity. "What many observers, who raise the risks of dismemberment underestimate in the case of Iraq," he says, "is the degree to which interests among various sections of the Iraqi population, especially, the more affluent and influential, are interlocked [so] that it would be very unlikely, though not impossible, to think of separate states within Iraq."

Iraqi political culture

The legacy of how Iraq was governed under the Ba'ath continues to shape attitudes and expectations today. Even more important than the state's use of violence was, in the opinion of Davis, its ambitious attempt to rewrite history and construct a new historical memory for Iraqis as a form of social control. According to him, "state-sponsored history writing and cultural production complement the state's use of violence in many important ways." Such memory harked back to the greatness of Iraq as the center of the Abbasid Empire and highlighted the role of Arab Sunnis. Appeals to pan-Arabism sought to reassure and elevate the Arab Sunnis, who were a minority in Iraq, but not in the Islamic world. This version of history promoted paranoia and xenophobia, and denigrated other groups (such as those of Persian descent) as less than fully Iraqi. It also incited suspicion of other states, especially Iran, maintaining that Iraq was often the victim of conspiracies that sought to thwart its progress.

The crushing and collapse of civil society under Saddam did not bode well for the resumption of political life in 2003. "…Authoritarian rule seriously undermined if not destroyed the institutions of civil society by atomizing the nation's populace and forcing associational activity underground or, more recently, to reconstitute itself beyond Iraq's boundaries," according to Davis. In the new Iraq, political parties have been regarded as vehicles for sectarian groups trying to impose their own agendas. So far they do not have a national or ideological appeal, as opposed to Iraqi political parties in the 1950s.

With the restoration of Iraqi sovereignty in June 2004, a domestic political process began which has exposed all of society's fault lines.

Elections were held for a 275-member Constituent Assembly in January 2005, which produced a new constitution calling for a weak federal system that was approved by referendum in October. This election was marked by voting along ethnic and sectarian lines, with a high turnout by Shi'i, excited at the prospect of taking power at last, and a boycott by Sunnis. The new Parliament elected in December 2005, however, was a disappointment, although Sunnis participated in the voting. The main characteristics of the new leaders were their inexperience, their domination by outsiders who had recently returned to Iraq, and their history of opposition to Saddam's government. All these factors led to an inability to work with each other, according to historian Phebe Marr. In May 2006, after months of bargaining, a national unity government was formed by Prime Minister Nuri al-Maliki, who was able to gradually consolidate power.

Despite the political progress, communal bloodletting worsened after the bombing of a major Shi'i mosque in Samarra, the Askariya Shrine (burial place of the 10th and 11th Shi'i Imams), in February 2006. The worst month of the war was December 2006, with about

SPENCER PLATT/GETTY IMAGES

Members of Montana's 163rd Alpha Company pose in front of an American flag on July 16, 2011, as they prepare to conclude their tour of duty in Iraq.

3,800 civilians killed, according to secret field reports released by WikiLeaks. From 2004 to 2009, there were over 100,000 civilian deaths.

Increased violence by Sunni Arab militia groups and al-Qaeda in Iraq starting in 2005, and mounting American casualties, led President Bush to announce in January 2007 that he would institute a troop increase (the "Surge"), which started taking effect in the summer of 2007 and by 2008 led to the decline in the level of violence. Part of the reason the Surge worked was the enlistment and bankrolling by the U.S. of armed Sunnis who had previously attacked U.S. forces. Formed into so-called "Awakening Councils" (Al Sahwa), these forces sought U.S. support in targeting al-Qaeda in Mesopotamia and Ba'athist groups who were attacking the coalition forces. Also, by this time, many areas had already been cleansed, and Iraqis had tired of the violence.

Endgame in Iraq

Once President Obama took office in 2009 he was immediately faced with the problem of implementing the plans of the Bush Administration to wind down the war. This was made easier by the decline in violence and in American casualties, not to mention the pressing need to focus on the "good war" in Afghanistan. By June 30, 2009, all U.S. troops had been withdrawn from Iraqi cities on schedule. By August 31, 2010, all combat troops were officially out of Iraq, and by the end of 2011 the remaining 50,000 U.S. troops—left to train Iraqi security forces, protect U.S. personnel and carry out counterterrorism operations—are supposed to be gone. These milestones were outlined in a status-of-forces agreement the Bush Administration reached with Iraq in late 2008. After the military departs, the State Department will oversee an estimated 6,000 to 7,000 contractors to provide protection and carry out many tasks formerly performed by U.S. troops, such as training the Iraqi police. Ironically, American companies are not playing a major role in reconstruction. The larger question, still unanswered in the fall of 2011, is whether and when the Iraqi Parliament will approve a new security agreement with the U.S. Many were apprehensive that, without the protection of U.S. troops, the country would collapse into civil war.

The most critical prerequisite for an American withdrawal is a functioning Iraqi government. In parliamentary elections of March 7, 2010, which were deemed fair, voting was largely along sectarian lines and an open-list system was used in which voters could choose individual candidates and not just a party. The winner by a hair was Ayad Allawi of the Al-Iraqiya Alliance. Allawi, a secular Shi'i, is a former prime minister with a Ba'athist past who won 91 of the 325 seats and got most of the Sunni and secular Shi'i vote. The prime minister, Nuri al-Maliki, a Shi'i of the State of Law Alliance, won 89 seats but was not ready to concede defeat. Another Shi'i group, the Islamic Supreme Council of Iraq (ISCI, formerly called SCIRI), representing the Hakim family, got 65 seats, including 40 for the Sadrists, and the Kurdish Alliance got 57 seats. According to Makiya, "Iraqi voters have come out well in this election. But they now have to contend with a political class that has proven itself to be both profoundly corrupt and capable of whipping up sectarian impulses whenever that seems to serve its interest."

Maliki was unwilling to accept the election results and nine months of tortuous negotiations followed until a new government was finally formed in December 2010. During this time decisionmaking was paralyzed and Iraqis grew more cynical about the democratic process. The big winners were Maliki himself, who remained as prime minister, and Muqtada al-Sadr, the young Shi'i firebrand whose decision (widely believed to be at Iranian direction) to throw in his lot with Maliki was the key to forming the government. The Kurdish parties maintained their previous position, with Jalal Talabani reelected as president by the Parliament. The Al-Iraqiya Alliance obtained the (weak) position of speaker of Parliament, and Allawi eventually turned down an offer to head a new strategic policy council, which he feared would be ineffective. For the first time, however, all the major political parties and ethnic groups are participating in the Parliament.

While Iraqis and outsiders were relieved that a national unity government was finally formed, its longevity is in question. By the summer of 2011 the government was under stress, with tensions among the ruling coalition, between Parliament and the executive branch and between the central and regional governments, according to an analysis by the

Carnegie Endowment for International Peace (CEIP). Prospects for successfully addressing pressing national issues are not high, due to Maliki's authoritarian streak and past readiness to fan sectarian issues. His government responded violently to protesters in major cities inspired by the Arab Spring who sought to object to corruption, mismanagement, lack of services and electricity, among other things.

Mission accomplished?

As the U.S. withdraws from Iraq, much that is left undone has aroused bitterness among Iraqis. High expectations on their part for better government services have not been met, and the country still has crippling power shortages, poor health care and an unresponsive and corrupt bureaucracy. "The dynamics of the political process in Iraq have evolved since 2003 in such a way as to put a very low premium on the idea of government service as a career or profession based on a disinterested view of the public good," according to Makiya.

The U.S. withdrawal from Iraq comes after almost a decade of massive expense and human sacrifice. Between 2003 and the end of 2010, the U.S. sustained 4,430 combat deaths, with 32,081 wounded, according to icasualties.org. A major "Costs of War" project carried out at Brown University, which released its findings in July 2011, estimated that the wars in Iraq, Afghanistan and Pakistan have cost the U.S. an estimated $3.2 trillion to $4 trillion. This includes not only the price of the military conflict, but also human costs that will continue far into the future, such as veterans' care, related foreign assistance, homeland security and interest payments—because these wars have been paid for almost entirely with borrowed money.

In December 2010, the UN Security Council removed most international sanctions placed on Iraq during the confrontation with Saddam. As an acknowledgment of political progress, Iraq is now permitted to develop a civilian nuclear program, the oil-for-food program was ended, and the country resumed control over most of its oil assets on June 30, 2011. Iraq has to continue setting aside 5% of its oil revenues as reparations for the damage done to Kuwait, which it still owes over $22 billion.

A number of critical issues still need to be resolved. Above all, the country needs good leadership and an effective Parliament that can achieve political consensus and promote national reconciliation. This will not come easily and certainly not soon. The balance of power between the center and the regions must be negotiated, including the degree of autonomy to allow the Kurds and the status of contested cities such as Kirkuk. There needs to be reconciliation between Shi'i and Sunnis, including the integration of Sunni forces in the Awakening Councils into the army, and an end to the exclusion from high positions of Sunnis who held minor Ba'athist affiliation. No law has yet been passed to regulate the distribution of Iraq's gas and oil revenues, which will be the major source of income in the future.

So far Iraqis have been too busy surviving the domestic turmoil to be focused on foreign policy. The future role of Iranian influence in Iraq is key. Ali Allawi, a former minister of finance, defense and trade, commented on "the visceral, almost atavistic, fears that the Arab nationalist, Sunni Arab political leadership and the insurgents had regarding Iran's motives and its supposely ubiquitous fifth columnists buried inside Iraqi society." While both countries have Shi'a governments there is a strong Iraqi nationalism that is suspicious of Iran's motives. Notably, the leading Shi'i cleric in Iraq, Ayatollah Ali Sistani, opposes an Islamic government along the lines of Iran. According to analyst Judith Yaphe of the National Defense University, "Conventional wisdom suggests that for the next five to ten years Iraqis will need to concentrate on reinventing themselves, their identity, their political institutions, and their economic infrastructure. For this endeavor, they will need cooperation from their neighbors in stabilizing trade and developing plans and maintaining secure borders. Future Iraqi governments, however, may have a different agenda." Eventually Iraq will re-arm, no doubt with U.S. aid, and this will alarm Iran and the Gulf states, who will have to reconfigure their relations once again.

As *The New York Times* editorialized, "The U.S. cannot fix Iraq. That is up to the Iraqis. But in the time left, this country has a responsibility and a strong strategic interest to do its best to help Iraq emerge from this disaster as a functioning, sovereign and reasonably democratic state."

4

The GCC: From Tribes to States

T<small>HE SIX</small> G<small>ULF MONARCHIES</small> have much in common, notably a heritage of tribal rule and vast petroleum resources, and have experienced the wrenching transformation of their societies in a headlong rush to modernize. The rapid transformation of Dubai, with features such as Burj Khalifa, the tallest building in the world, and the saga of the city's recent economic crash, are now legendary. Yet not everything in the former Trucial Coast has changed: "Attitudes, values, behaviour and customs which were formed under quite different circumstances continue to be essential to the family's life," according to Frauke Heard-Bey, the leading historian of the UAE. Due to their disparity in size and population with neighboring states, they are acutely aware of their vulnerability. Fear of Iran and Iraq led to the formation of their union in 1981, and since that time they have openly sought Western protection. As a reaction to the threat posed by the Arab Spring revolts, suggestions were made to have Jordan and Morocco join the GCC, although it is unclear if this will happen.

The persistence of monarchy

Monarchies have fallen all over the Middle East since World War II, the conspicuous exceptions being the GCC states, plus Jordan and Morocco. (There are actually 12 ruling families in the Gulf, including 7 in the UAE.) This has led to a lively debate among political scientists as to what accounts for such longevity. Many have proposed that it is due to unique cultural factors in the Gulf, including a paternalistic tribal tradition in which many of the states have been ruled by the same family for two-and-a-half centuries. The rulers have been astute in balancing competing internal and external interests, and in creating a "national myth" that legitimizes their power. In the opinion of Professor Gause, monarchy has endured as the form of government there mainly because of external factors—the protection of outside powers and income from oil revenues. The development of the rentier state, along with small and relatively homogeneous populations, gave them an extended lease on life.

Whether the Persian Gulf states are an exception to the world-wide trend toward greater democratization is an issue much debated by scholars of the region. It is true that the GCC countries have no free press (except perhaps Kuwait), no real political parties and few trade unions, and abuses of guest workers are rife. Government traditionally has bought off or suppressed potential opposition. The "private sector" in the Gulf is based on kinship relations and works closely with the government to maintain a favored position. It may have neither the power nor the inclination to force major changes in nondemocratic political regimes.

Political change in the Arabian peninsula has been clearly linked to a new generation taking power, Oman and Qatar being good examples. The issue of succession is critical, if little discussed in public. The current ruler of Kuwait assumed office in 2006; of Saudi Arabia in 2005; of the UAE in 2004; of Bahrain in 1999; of Qatar in 1995; and of Oman in 1970.

In Saudi Arabia only sons of Ibn Sa'ud, the country's founder who died in 1953, have ruled, and passing the throne to the next generation could prove momentous. A 1992 edict opened the succession to Ibn Sa'ud's grandsons, meaning scores of princes are now eligible, although "the most upright" is to be chosen. It also specified that the king could choose and remove the crown prince, so holding this office does not guarantee succession.

The current ruler, King Abdullah, is 87 years old, and has effectively ruled since 1995 when his brother was incapacitated by a stroke. Abdullah has worked to foster a more tolerant environment, restraining radical clerics, revising textbooks, making an overture to the Shi'i, and pursuing an antiterrorism policy. The idea of reform has been debated in Saudi for the past few years, but progress has been slow due to caution by Abdullah, struggle between reformers and conservatives and tepid public support. The succession is not far off and it is unclear what policies a successor would follow.

Political reform

Until recently, the most significant fact about political reform in the Gulf states is that it has come from the top, not the bottom, and is aimed at preserving the power of the ruling families. "An overarching theme is that change has consistently been initiated by the elites themselves and has taken the character of controlled liberalization rather than a substantive shift in power relationships. A process of democratization, therefore, has not been established," according to Professors Anoushiravan Ehteshami and Steven Wright. There is also a "culture of deference" in the region that may inhibit challenging authority, notes Prof. Gerd Nonneman of Georgetown University. This is not to say that all change is resisted; regimes need to be seen as legitimate to help preserve stability, especially because of their close ties to the U.S. Only Kuwait allows real politics, with struggle between the executive and legislative branches. A decision to permit this in the other Gulf monarchies would be an important milestone in empowering civil society, although the first to benefit would probably be Islamist groups.

The Gulf monarchies are all reforming at different rates. They clearly see their fate as linked and will be influenced by each other's experiences with greater political liberalization. Thus the GCC Ministerial Council that met in Manama, Bahrain, on February 17, 2011, pledged full support for the Bahraini government's crackdown on the protesters. Kuwait has gone the farthest, with regular elections and a Parliament that relishes interrogating ministers. (The Kuwaiti prime minister, a member of the royal family, barely survived a no-confidence vote in December 2010.) In 2005, women in Kuwait won the right to vote, and in May 2009, four women were elected to Parliament, a first in the Gulf. After the death of the emir in December 2005, the Parliament insisted on playing a role in choosing his successor, overruling the decision of the Al Sabah family.

The need for reform has become more obvious in the context of the Arab Spring. Abdulaziz Sager, chairman of the Gulf Research Center in Dubai, warned in April 2011 that "if the ruling families of the Gulf want to maintain their legitimacy, they need to adapt quickly to the changing times and enact substantive political reform that reflects their people's aspirations. Time is no longer on their side. If they wait too long, their rule cannot be assured."

The Al Sa'ud are skilled at balancing the demands of many sectors, and have "a proven record of pragmatism and adaptability, with skill at co-optation," Professors Paul Aarts and Gerd Nonneman wrote in 2005. They concluded that "while it seems likely that Saudi Arabia will move further in the direction of liberalisation, it is...unlikely that it will move beyond the confines of 'liberalized autocracy' for at least a generation." The Arab Spring protests alarmed the Saudi leadership, but they were still not prepared to introduce real reform. Their main response was to ramp up the politics of patronage, with major spending ($130 billion) allocated to the creation of new jobs, housing, a higher minimum wage and increased support for religious institutions, notes Steffen Hertog of the LSE. The Wahhabi ulama expressed their support for the state, warning that demonstrations

Saudi Shi'i protesters hold Saudi flags and portraits of unidentified prisoners during a demonstration in Qatif, Saudi Arabia, on March 9, 2011.

are forbidden. Calls for a "Day of Rage" to be held on March 11 elicited little response, except for small protests in the Shi'i-majority eastern part of the country. According to Prof. Stéphane Lacroix of the Institut d'Études Politiques de Paris (Sciences Po), "The real reason that Saudi Arabia has not seen major protests is that the Saudi regime has effectively co-opted the Sahwa, the powerful Islamist network which would have to play a major role in any sustained mobilization of protests." The prospect of increased clerical power is a cause for concern.

Gulf economies today

The economies of these rentier states are almost completely dependent on income from the sale of oil and gas, although it should be noted that they have also created a large number of profitable and efficient state-owned enterprises. During the first oil boom, which lasted from 1973 to 1982, and the second one, from 2003 to 2008, the revenues were extraordinary. But these revenues have fluctuated wildly in recent years. There is a big difference in the amount of petroleum reserves and thus income among the GCC states and even within the UAE; for example, Bahrain and Oman are projected to run out of oil by 2025. According to the *CIA World Factbook*, per capita gross domestic product (GDP) in 2010 amounted to $179,000 in Qatar, $49,600 (UAE), $48,900 (Kuwait), $40,300 (Bahrain), $25,600 (Oman), $24,200 (Saudi Arabia) $10,600 (Iran) and $3,800 (Iraq). The figure for the U.S. is $47,200.

At the end of 2010, Saudi Arabia ranked first in proven reserves, with 265 billion barrels, followed by Iran (137 billion), Iraq (115 billion), Kuwait (102 billion), the UAE (98 billion), Qatar (26 billion) and Oman (6 billion). The cost of oil production in the Gulf is the lowest in the world: It currently ranges from $1.50 to $6 a barrel in Saudi Arabia, while a gallon of gasoline costs under 15 cents to produce. The Gulf is also rich in natural gas, with Iran and Qatar holding the world's second- and third-largest reserves, respectively.

Finding a balance between oil supply and demand has always been a challenge. On the one hand, oil companies need a price high enough to fund research and exploration, and investment in alternative energy sources must be financially attractive. On the other, economic growth needs to be maintained and consumers must be able to afford the product.

How significant is U.S. reliance on imported oil? In 2010, the U.S. depended on imports for 49.3% of its energy needs, the first time in a decade this number had fallen below 50%. U.S. imports from the Middle East also have declined relative to other areas. "Energy independence" has been a goal of the U.S. since the Nixon Administration (1969-74), but has never been achieved.

Since the oil price shocks of 1973 and 1979 that led to sharply higher prices, the world has been fixated on the price of oil. In the 1990s, it was about $25 a barrel, but prices rose dramatically from 2003 to mid-2008. In a period of volatile swings, oil went from a peak of $145 a barrel in the summer of 2008 to a low point of $33 in December 2008. After mid-2009 the price of oil stabilized in the $70 to $80 range, which seemed to be a "sweet spot" for both producers and consumers. By the summer of 2011, with prices hovering around $100 a barrel, demand strong and supplies tight, Saudi Arabia was unable to persuade OPEC to raise production levels and vowed to do so itself.

A key question affecting price is future demand. Due to the worsening economic outlook, in August 2011 the top three forecasters, the International Energy Agency, OPEC and the Energy Information Administration (EIA), a U.S. governent agency, all lowered their estimates for oil demand in 2012. However, supplies still remain tight and unless there are production increases, prices will remain high. The EIA expects the average cost of crude oil for U.S. refiners to rise from $100 per barrel in 2011 to $103 per barrel in 2012, with demand in 2011 estimated at 88.2 million barrels a day (mmb/d) and 89.6 mmb/d in 2012.

The crash of Dubai

The global downturn hit the Gulf with a vengeance as the roaring economy of Dubai, built on real estate speculation and tourism, started unraveling in the fall of 2008. Producing little oil, Dubai relied on its reputation as a trading center with few restrictions to attract capital and talent from around the world. Over-the-top projects, such as the world's tallest building, a seven-star hotel, and an indoor ski slope, set the tone of unbridled consumption. Tourists wearing provocative attire and the wide availability of alcohol and prostitutes were an affront to local sensibilities. It became apparent that the "Dubai model" was a mirage that could not be maintained, and by the end of 2008 the government, which shunned transparency, admitted it had a debt of $80 billion (in October 2010 a poll of economists put the true figure at $115 billion). "This economic collapse was taking place against an increasingly unpleasant backdrop of corruption, authoritarianism and protectionism," according to Christopher M. Davidson of Britain's Durham University. "The 'Dubai vision' was never more than a giant gamble, most of it with other people's money." Only Abu Dhabi has the funds to bail out Dubai, but has been slow to do so, and in return may impose closer control over the freewheeling lifestyle there and crack down on its close ties with Iran. Abu Dhabi is now discouraging Iranians and Shi'i in general from settling in the UAE. As a result of the world economic slowdown, two thirds of those working in the Gulf did not receive a pay raise in 2009, and about 10% of professionals working in the GCC lost their jobs. There has been an exodus of expatriates and by October 2010 some 400,000 laborers had left. The economic situation is now beginning to stabilize, partly thanks to high oil prices, but the debt crisis is far from resolved and further restructuring and asset sales are expected.

Demographic trends

As in the rest of the region, the GCC states are experiencing a "youth bulge." In 2010, the proportion of the population under the age of 15 in Bahrain was 20%; in Kuwait, 23%; in Oman, 29%; in Qatar, 15%; in Saudi Arabia, 38%; and in the UAE, 19% (in the U.S. it is 20% and in Europe 16%). The rapidly growing indigenous populations are putting pressure on governments to provide jobs, but many youth are not receiving an education that provides the skills needed in a modern society–especially in Saudi Arabia due to the emphasis on religious education. This forces countries to outsource many of the best jobs. There is a strong preference on the part of nationals to work for the government, as working in the public sector assures them of higher wages, shorter working hours and longer holidays, plus the likelihood that they will not be fired.

Globalization and the Gulf

Today, new technologies are playing an important role in opening up Gulf societies to the outside world, and this has tended to undermine the rulers' monopoly of power. Starting with fax, satellite TV and e-mail, and now mobile phones, VoIP, SMS and social networks such as Twitter, Facebook and YouTube, people in the Gulf states can connect through a variety of means that were not available 20 years ago. Governments long used to controlling the flow of information are uncomfortable about this, but they recognize it is inevitable and even necessary for businesses to compete. They monitor it so that nothing "un-Islamic" is transmitted, meaning in practice pornography and religious or political material.

One of the best examples of how the new media are transforming the dialogue between citizens and rulers in the Gulf is the "Twitter Revolution" in Iran in the summer of 2009, a tactic which was later utilized to mobilize protesters in Tunisia and Egypt. In the summer of 2010, attempts by the UAE and Saudi Arabia to censor Black-Berry use caused a whirlwind of protest, especially among business users and expatriates who relied on these devices to get their jobs done. Governments, however, fear giving domestic critics, let alone terrorists, free use of encrypted communications.

A major development was the start of broadcasting in November

Dubai's 160-story Burj Khalifa, the world's tallest tower, is named after the ruler of Abu Dhabi, which bailed out Dubai in the 2009 debt crisis.

1996 by Al Jazeera, the Arabic satellite channel based in Qatar that has fearlessly aired regional problems and criticized most leaders in the Middle East. Al Jazeera profoundly changed the media environment, according to French journalist Olivier Da Lage: "State broadcasting authorities, and newspaper managers in the Middle East, international broadcasters elsewhere, and governments in the region and beyond had to rethink their policies, change the way they addressed their people and the people of their neighboring countries." Al Jazeera played a major role in covering the unrest in Tunisia, Egypt and Libya, but was criticized for holding back when it came to protests in Bahrain, Oman and Saudi Arabia.

Use of the internet is soaring and Web sites have proliferated in the region. According to Internet World Stats, a website that tracks usage, as of March 2011 Iran had by far the largest number of internet users (over 33 million) in the region, with user growth from

This picture shows a sweeping view inside the headquarters of Al Jazeera's television network in Doha, Qatar.

2000 to 2010 an astonishing 13,000%. The internet penetration of the Gulf population is high: UAE, 69%, Qatar, 67%, Bahrain, 54%, Oman, 48%, Saudi Arabia, 44%, Iran, 47%, Kuwait, 42%, with Iraq far behind at 3% (numbers rounded).

Guest workers

When the dramatic rise of oil revenues in the 1970s enabled the Gulf states to carry out major construction and modernization projects, Gulf states brought in outside workers because of the shortage of local manpower. Labor migration in the 1950s and 1960s came mainly from neighboring Arab states, whereas Asian workers had been preferred in the 1970s and 1980s. Since about 1990, Gulf states have tried to reduce the presence of foreign workers and nationalize operations. In the wake of the Gulf War, there was a large-scale expulsion of Arab migrant workers thought to be politically unreliable, including Palestinians, Jordanians, Yemenis and Sudanese. Gulf states now prefer hiring Asians rather than Arabs, since they are easier to control and willing to work for less, and those in low-end jobs do not bring their families. For them, salaries are much higher than at home, and remittances from the Gulf, amounting to $40 billion in 2008, are of critical importance to the economies of receiving countries, especially in South Asia. Pakistan alone received $6.5 billion in remittances from the Gulf in the 2010–11 financial year.

This process has led to a major imbalance in numbers between nationals and guest workers, and strained relations between the two. In 2010, at least 17 million expatriates lived in the GCC. In 2008, foreigners accounted for 90% of the labor force in the UAE, 86% in Qatar, 83% in Kuwait, 65% in Saudi Arabia and Oman, and 62% in Bahrain. Some of these expatriate workers have spent much of their lives there, yet it is practically impossible for them to gain citizenship.

In the Gulf these workers span the spectrum from professionals who do much of the managerial and office work and are relatively well-off, to those on the bottom who are exploited for manual labor—men in construction and women as household help. In both cases they are vulnerable, feel discriminated against, live lives apart from nationals and have little social interaction with them. The constant threat of violence and even deportation hangs over them. A central mechanism of control is the *kafala,* or system of sponsorship that is necessary to live and work in the Arab Gulf states. The worker is dependent on his or her sponsor, who has the power to obtain residence permits, guarantee continued employment and confiscate passports. (Recently, Bahrain and Kuwait have made reforms in the kafala system, moving it from an employer-based to a government-based system, but the outcome is unclear.)

The plight of migrant construction workers in the UAE came to world attention when it was highlighted in a major report by Human Rights Watch in November 2006, "Building Towers, Cheating Workers." Some half a million construction workers, mainly from India, Pakistan and Bangladesh, built modern Dubai, yet were subject to abuses such as low or unpaid wages, hazardous working conditions leading to death or injury, the withholding of passports and high indebtedness to recruiting agencies. They are not allowed to form trade unions. A sizeable minority have gone home due to the economic downturn and increased opportunities in India. After the bad publicity, Dubai shut over 100 camps and has tried to get employers to upgrade accommodations.

Although in the past Gulf cities were noted for their cosmopolitanism, the states have now drawn a sharp line between the pampered nationals who receive jobs, housing subsidies, free health care and a myriad of other benefits, and the supposedly temporary workers. In major cities such as Dubai and Doha visitors quickly realize that nationals are in the minority. Only citizens are permitted to wear "national dress," which they prefer as a mark of citizenship and privilege. The number of Asian expatriates is thought to be a threat to local culture and to the vitality of the Arabic language. "Though there is no real evidence of a security threat," according to political analyst N. Janardhan, "some are warning that 'guest workers' are a 'time bomb waiting to explode.'" The question of national identity has become espe-

An Indian laborer, one of many guest workers in the UAE, in front of a building site in Dubai, whose skyline is under construction.

cially acute in the UAE. In the opinion of Janardhan, "the GCC countries need to rid themselves of their obsessive preoccupation with defensive demographic strategies and introduce new policy instruments to tackle their problems."

The balance of fear

One of the results of the collapse of Iraq has been an increased awareness in the Gulf of destabilizing transnational forces that pose a threat to ruling dynasties, such as tension between Arabs and Persians, Sunni/Shi'i differences, and terrorism on the part of extreme Islamist groups. Protected by an implicit U.S. security umbrella against outside attack, internal threats to regime security have become the prime concern.

Overlaying regional politics is tension between Arab and Persian, rooted in longstanding mutual perceptions. A frequent reminder of this is the lexical struggle over the term "Persian Gulf" or "Arabian Gulf." Large numbers of people of Persian heritage live on the Arab coast, especially big merchants in Bahrain and Dubai, where they play an important economic role. An estimated 450,000 Iranians live in the UAE alone, where there are 8,000 Iranian companies. The reexport trade to Iran has risen steadily, officially reaching over $8.5 billion in 2010. Likewise many ethnic Arabs live on the Iranian shoreline (some have migrated to take jobs in GCC states) and in the southwest province of Khuzistan.

A 'Crescent of Crisis'?

Probably a more important distinction than ethnicity in the Gulf is religion, in this case Sunni and Shi'i Islam. Shi'is make up an estimated 87% of the population in Iran, 73% in Bahrain, 25% in Saudi Arabia, 23% in Kuwait, 19% in Qatar, 9% in the UAE, and 5% in Oman, according to figures accompanying the map, "Persian Gulf Region: Religious Composition," located at http://gulf2000. columbia.edu/. (These numbers are subject to dispute. For example, the government of Bahrain has tried to tip the demographic balance by granting citizenship to many Sunnis—particularly in the security and defense forces—from places like Pakistan, Yemen, Syria and Jordan, perhaps reducing the Shi'i majority to 60%. In the case of Saudi Arabia smaller numbers such as 10% to 15% are usually cited, which do not include Shi'i communities in the western part of the country.)

The U.S. occupation of Iraq changed the religious balance of power in the region. "By liberating and empowering Iraq's Shi'i majority, the Bush Administration helped launch a broad Shi'i revival that will upset the sectarian balance in Iraq and the Middle East for years to come," according to Prof. Vali Nasr of Tufts University. Rulers of neighboring states with significant Shi'i populations such as Saudi Arabia, Bahrain and Kuwait were alarmed. They feared increased Iranian influence in the Middle East and new demands for political and social recognition on the part of their own Shi'i minorities. In December 2004 King Abdullah of Jordan warned that if the new Iraqi government fell under Iranian influence, a "crescent" of Shi'i movements would result, threatening Sunni governments as well as posing a problem for U.S. interests. Former Egyptian President Mubarak, reflecting usually unstated anxieties, said in April 2005 that "Shiites are mostly always loyal to Iran and not the countries where they live."

After the fall of Saddam, the transnational connections of the Shi'i were reinvigorated and thousands can now make the pilgrimage to Iraqi holy cities. However, many analysts conclude that fears of a rising "Shi'i crescent" are misplaced. For one thing, the Shi'i community is not unified but divided, with many clerics competing for leadership. The most prominent cleric outside Iran at present is Ali Sistani in Iraq, whom many Arab Shi'i in the Gulf emulate.

In the Gulf states, Iranian influence is much more limited than in Iraq or Lebanon, according to French scholar Laurence Louër. Shi'is in the Gulf have sought to demonstrate loyalty to their own states rather than Iran. Louër found that Shi'i movements in the Arab Gulf states were offshoots of Iraqi (not Iranian) movements, and there was a division between pro- and anti-Iranian Shi'is. The change of government in Iraq in 2003 did lead to an improvement of the lot of Gulf Shi'i that has been under way since the 1990s. Arab governments have sought to co-opt Iranian influence by granting some rights, such as public observance of Ashura rituals, tolerated in Kuwait and Saudi Arabia since 2004. In Dubai, Iranian immigrants were traditionally welcomed and free to worship, do business and make money. The situation in Bahrain differs. The Shi'i have been largely free to practice their religion, but prevented from achieving the political dominance their numbers would suggest. This is a major grievance in the ongoing strife there.

The Islamic opposition in Saudi Arabia

The resurgence of religion in personal and political life that has marked the Middle East since the 1970s seemed to have hardly touched the Arabian peninsula. After all, Saudi Arabia was the most "Islamic" of states, being the birthplace of Islam and strictly ruled according to the Sharia, or Islamic law. However, in the Muslim world political action has always been taken in the name of religion by governments and opposition groups alike. In 1979,

Saudi security forces fought a bloody battle to oust Islamic militants who had taken over Islam's holiest site, the Great Mosque in Mecca, in a protest over the rule of the Al Sa'ud. After that time, the state lavished attention on the Wahhabi ulama and there was little evidence of opposition activity.

The second Gulf War changed everything and led to the rise of a potent Islamist opposition. "The post-war resurgence of Islamism was a reaffirmation of identity, a protest movement against the monarchy and its Western allies, and for some, a means to achieve social influence and, perhaps, a takeover of power," according to political scientist R. Hrair Dekmejian. A new generation of clerics known as the "Sahwa" (Awakening) led resistance to state policies. They accused the ruling Al Sa'ud of squandering resources, being puppets of the West and not being sufficiently "Islamic" in their rule. A bitter split developed between the "official" religious establishment supported by the state and the regime critics. Thus the *fatwa* or ruling allowing non-Muslim forces to enter Saudi Arabia in 1990, issued by the senior religious scholar, Shaikh Abd al-Aziz bin Baz, was criticized as a sellout on the part of some Wahhabi ulama.

The Islamic opposition took a more ominous turn with the bombings of an American military training mission in Riyadh in November 1995 and the attack in June 1996 on an American residential compound in Dhahran. Then bin Laden founded a transnational Islamist network, al-Qaeda, based in Afghanistan, which carried out the attacks of September 11, 2001. (Many were shocked that 15 of the 19 airplane hijackers were identified as Saudi.) Efforts to launch an insurgency in Saudi Arabia by an offshoot, al-Qaeda in the Arabian Peninsula (AQAP), led to violent incidents between 2003 and 2006. After a devastating attack on three housing complexes in Riyadh in May 2003, the Saudi government began a serious crackdown on terrorism and warned radical clerics to get in line.

By 2008, the attempt to carry out jihad in Saudi Arabia had proven to be a failure, according to terrorism expert Thomas

Hegghammer. The AQAP campaign failed because it lacked popular support, was subjected to an increased government crackdown and suffered a split among jihadists, some of whom gave priority to struggle in war zones such as Iraq and Afghanistan. A new Yemeni branch of al-Qaeda has been active since 2006, and assumed the AQAP name in 2009, but has little in common with its namesake. In light of the killing of bin Laden and the fact that Islamist demands did not motivate the Arab Spring protests, some analysts feel that support for al-Qaeda may be in decline. The Obama Administration regards AQAP as the most immediate threat to the U.S. homeland, although a U.S. missile strike killed Anwar al-Awlaki, a radical American-born cleric and prominent advocate of jihad living in Yemen, on September 30, 2011.

How dangerous is the Islamic opposition in Saudi Arabia? At present it is more an annoyance to the ruling family than a real threat. The Al Sa'ud can count on the support of the Wahhabi ulama, revel in their custody of the holy sites in the Hijaz and have vast financial resources at their disposal. The legitimacy of the royal family to rule is well-established and religiously justified, and the unrest in Iraq has made Saudis think twice about replacing their government. However, the strict Wahhabi interpretation of Islam has little appeal in the Hijaz or Shi'i parts of the country. Nor does it appeal to the modern middle class.

A more recent concern is how winding down the war in Iraq will affect Saudi Arabia. A classified memo sent by Secretary of State Hillary Clinton in December 2009, revealed by WikiLeaks, concluded that "donors in Saudi Arabia constitute the most significant source of funding to Sunni terrorist groups worldwide." The sectarian bloodletting and exclusion of Sunnis from high office in Iraq has led to concern for their safety, and Saudi money has likely helped finance the Sunni rebellion there. The Iraq conflict has served as a destination of Saudi jihadists, who have gone there to fight against the Shi'i and the Americans. The Saudi government fears that these forces will receive training and experience, only to later return home and foment instability.

The revolt in Bahrain

Bahrain has had a somewhat different political trajectory than the other GCC states, due to the makeup of its population, its negligible oil wealth and significant British intervention in its internal affairs prior to independence. Here, as in Iraq before 2003, a Sunni ruling family presides over a state that is two-thirds Shi'i. The ruling Al Khalifah are not prepared to allow genuine democracy as it would surely end their control. While the Shi'i have the right to worship, they are marginalized economically and politically and not allowed to serve in the military. Shi'is resent accusations by the government that their true loyalty lies with Iran. When King Hamad b. Isa Al Khalifah assumed rule in 1999, he did introduce some reforms, but unemployment, inflation, poverty and disappointment at the lack of political progress fostered a new antigovernment rebellion, which has become much worse than the one that festered between 1994 and 1999. A major security crackdown on Shi'i activists in advance of October 2010 elections further poisoned the atmosphere.

Major demonstrations broke out in February 2011 in solidarity with protesters in Egypt. Bahraini protesters demanded an end to corruption, accountability on the part of the government, better education and housing and a revision of the constitution. The opposition was not sectarian—Sunnis also participated—but Shi'is were in the forefront as they have suffered the brunt of discrimination. The government, however, framed the conflict as a Shi'i/Sunni one backed by Iran. On March 14, 2011, it invited in an estimated 1,000 troops from Saudi Arabia and 500 police from the UAE, under GCC auspices, to cow the protesters and impose order. On March 18 it cracked down brutally, dispersing protesters gathered at Pearl Square and tearing down the 300-foot sculpture in its center that had become the symbol of the movement. Martial law was in effect until June 1.

Once known as the most liberal state in the Gulf, Bahrain was accused of serious human rights violations including the arbitrary detention of over a thousand people and long prison sentences for protest leaders. Income from business, especially banking, and tourism, fell off drastically. The U.S., whose Fifth Fleet is based there,

After clashing with riot police, protesters celebrate the retaking of Pearl Square in Manama, Bahrain, on February 19, 2011.

muted its public criticism. "The Saudi intervention, however small, is … a major step backward for the region. It represents a major slap in the face to the United States, a defeat for the liberal Shiite and Sunni elements in Bahrain, and ultimately a catastrophe for the entire Khalifa family, both the liberal and conservative wings, who may have just surrendered their power to the giant next door," in the opinion of Jean-François Seznec of Georgetown University. The International Crisis Group (ICG) warned in April that the crackdown and foreign intervention "could turn a mass movement for democratic reform into an armed conflict while regionalising a genuinely internal political struggle." A "National Dialogue" that was supposed to lead to reconciliation took place in July, but did not achieve much. The ruling family did not take part, and the main Shi'i opposition party, al-Wefaq, walked out. Afterward, the king

81

approved parliamentary reforms but maintained royal control of the upper house. "There is reason to fear that Bahrain is heading for prolonged political stalemate, enforced by a heavy security presence backed by foreign troops and punctuated by protests when circumstance permits," in the opinion of Robert Malley of the ICG.

Gulf security

The states that now make up the GCC have long sought protection by an outside power, at first the British and later the Americans. They are accustomed to outsourcing their defense needs—at great expense—which has led all of them to reach written or unwritten defense agreements with the U.S. It has also led to a correct, if sometimes contentious, relationship with Iran. As memorably put by the Qatari prime minister to the U.S. ambassador in December 2009 and revealed by WikiLeaks, "They lie to us; we lie to them." The Gulf royals have generally avoided taking risky actions that could antagonize their neighbors, and the smaller states sometimes feel like they are being bullied by Saudi Arabia, which hinders regional cooperation and integration. In all the GCC states, regime survival is the key.

Iranian threats to close the Strait of Hormuz or retaliate against targets in the Gulf if attacked have been very unsettling. In addition to this, there were renewed suggestions in August 2008 on the part of the deputy foreign minister that the Gulf monarchies lacked legitimacy, which seemed a throwback to 30 years ago when Iran sought to export its revolution. The Gulf rulers in particular fear Iran's nuclear program, especially in light of the nuclear fiasco in Japan. They have asserted that they also have a right to nuclear technology for peaceful purposes. Saudi Arabia and the UAE are in the early stages of developing nuclear power, mainly for desalination and production of electricity, while others fear an arms race in the region. Iran has long advocated a security regime that would include only the regional states, but there is no realistic prospect the GCC states will agree unless there is a change of government in Tehran and the agreement is broadened to include other states.

Border disputes

One of the main sources of instability in the Gulf region is unresolved border and boundary disputes, largely arising from the colonial powers' redrawing the map of the Middle East after World War I. Such disputes, however, are increasingly being settled, partly in order to facilitate oil operations. One of the most dramatic examples came in March 2001, when Bahrain and Qatar accepted the verdict of the World Court that settled their longstanding territorial dispute, largely in favor of the former.

Even when "solved," disputes over borders tend to break out anew when political conditions change or tension rises between states. For example, the UAE border with Saudi Arabia was supposedly settled in 1974, when the Saudis were granted a strip of coastline on the Gulf at the base of the Khor al-Udaid inlet that had previously connected the UAE to Qatar. This agreement was contested after the accession of Shaikh Khalifah in the UAE in 2004, and was not finally resolved until March 2009, when it was agreed to revert to the original treaty. Also a matter of dispute has been the giant oil field on the border between the UAE (where it is known as Zarrara) and Saudi Arabia (where it is known as Shaybah), which allocates the entire output to Saudi. In another example, Iran and Qatar share a huge gas field in the Gulf (called the North Field by Qatar and South Pars by Iran). This may lead to future disputes, as Qatar has become a major liquefied natural gas (LNG) exporter, while Iran still lacks the technology to produce any.

A key problem blocking regional détente is the century-long dispute between Iran and the UAE over the sovereignty of three tiny islands, Abu Musa and the two Tunbs, at the mouth of the Gulf. These islands were occupied by force by Iran in 1971 in the wake of the British withdrawal. Iran regarded itself as entitled to assert control, since it had already made a concession to the Arab states by relinquishing its claim to Bahrain in 1970. A Memorandum of Understanding was signed between Iran and Sharjah agreeing to jointly administer Abu Musa. In

1992 the issue, dormant for two decades, flared up, due to Iran's militarization of the islands on the one hand and, on the other, the UAE's contention that Iran is an illegal occupier. Iran has repeatedly appealed to the UAE to negotiate the future of Abu Musa, while the UAE has so far refused unless the matter of the Tunbs is also addressed. Iran regards the issue of the Tunbs as settled and has rejected the UAE's suggestion to take the dispute to the World Court.

The UAE's strategy has been to internationalize the issue, and it has been successful in gaining support within Arab forums such as the GCC and the Arab League. Both regularly denounce the "Iranian occupation" of the islands. The problem is that both sides have become hemmed in by overblown rhetoric on the value of the islands and the murky historical claims of both to them. The dispute over these islands, in the opinion of geographer Richard Schofield of King's College (London), has now become primarily a symbolic one, activated at times of Arab-Iranian tension, which can be managed but is not likely to have final legal resolution.

Environmental stress

Although "environmental degradation and climate change barely feature in regional security discourse," they may increasingly do so in the future, according to Dr. Ulrichsen of LSE. The Gulf is unusual among the world's seas in being shallow, hot and salty, as well as almost cut off from other bodies of water. The annual rate of evaporation far exceeds the amount of rainfall, and the temperature of Gulf waters is projected to rise between 3° and 6°C during the 21st century. Because of this many animal species living there are at the upper limit of their ability to adapt. Still, the Gulf harbors a rich and valuable fauna, including, most notably, pearl oysters, as well as shrimp and many kinds of fish, such as the prized grouper (*hamour*).

Since the development of petroleum resources in the 20th century, the Gulf has become highly vulnerable to pollution from tanker traffic. The war against Iraq in early 1991 was particularly hard on the regional environment. Iraqi forces occupying Kuwait discharged 6 million to 8 million gallons of oil into the Gulf, creating the largest oil spill in the world, covering over 600 square miles and severely affecting marine life. Hundreds of miles of the Saudi coast between al-Khafji and al-Jubail were coated in tar and the intertidal zone was severely affected, although in deeper waters the damage appears to have been much less. Before they left Kuwait, Iraqi troops set almost 800 oil wells on fire, spewing black smoke over the area, and creating around 300 oil lakes, covering 30 square miles. Another major problem is vessels flushing their tanks before loading new cargo, which discharges oil into the Gulf and is hard to detect since it is often done at night.

The extensive desalination facilities now critical to Gulf cities are under continuous threat from oil spills. Although there are no plants in Iran or Iraq, the GCC states (except for Oman and Saudi Arabia) depend on them almost exclusively for freshwater. The rapid urbanization that has taken place has led to unprecedented demands for water and put great stress on ecosystems. The UAE, for example, is notorious for having the highest per capita use of

INTERNATIONAL SPACE STATION/NASA

Dubai's Palm Island Resort seen in 2005, when it was under construction.

water in the world. Consumers have little incentive to conserve water, and there is only a four-day supply in reserve. The construction of fanciful artificial islands off Dubai, like the Palm Jumeirah, built on top of a coral reef, also has had a highly detrimental impact on the environment.

The GCC states are now very alarmed about the environmental impact of the Iranian nuclear reactor producing electricity at Bushire, directly across the Gulf from Kuwait. There is concern that Gulf waters could be polluted by radioactive leakage, which due to prevailing winds and currents would soon reach the southern shore. Any contamination of the oil fields or desalination plants would be catastrophic. Aside from any system failure, the reactor is built in an earthquake zone and neighboring states fear it is a disaster waiting to happen.

$$\gg \circ \ll$$

The GCC states are small, rich and vulnerable, and will likely require continued outside protection. In an age of globalization, internal and external security threats have become closely intertwined in the Gulf, and governments must find new ways to cope with them. In the wake of political change in Egypt and the pro-democracy fervor sweeping the Arab world, the GCC monarchs feel besieged and seek to stick together. The biggest challenge for the monarchs is to reinforce their own legitimacy to rule while carefully expanding political space. Resisting supposed Iranian influence and meddling is also a top priority. Finding a satisfactory status for the supposedly temporary guest workers who now constitute the bulk of the workforce is also essential. If oil revenues remain high, they may continue to buy off dissent. If the price of oil should collapse once again, these rentier states would be in big trouble. All of them need to contemplate a post-oil future.

5

Iran: The Revolution Continues

THE SURPRISE ELECTION of Mahmoud Ahmadinejad as president in 2005, and his contested re-election in 2009, led to massive protests and bitter political infighting in Iran, heightened regional tensions and caused a confrontation with the U.S. It also set Iran on a very different course than that charted by his predecessor, Mohammad Khatami. Khatami's landslide election in 1997 had marked a new phase in Iran's transition to a postrevolutionary era. Iranians, especially women and youth, enthusiastically backed his call for moderation, tolerance and the rule of law. Khatami stood for change, and he was propelled by a surge of "people power" not seen since the revolution. He reflected the hopes of a new generation disillusioned by the revolution's unmet promises.

One of President Khatami's most cherished goals was that a civil society should develop in Iran. His government fostered a discourse on the rule of law, civil rights and social freedom, which encouraged

Iranians to express their opinions more openly than previously possible. A liberal press blossomed, and a burst of creativity in filmmak-
ing led to worldwide acclaim for Iranian motion pictures. Iranian
expectations for the future were high. In terms of foreign policy,
there was steady movement away from an emphasis on ideology
to that of national interest. Iran markedly improved relations with
Western Europe and with its neighbors in the Persian Gulf.

Despite popular support, however, strong conservative forces were
arrayed against Khatami and the advocates of reform, and by the end
of his second term in 2005 the reform movement lay in ruins. The
"parallel government" of unelected institutions, including the *Rahbar*
(Leader), Ayatollah Ali Khamenei, the security forces, the judiciary
and broadcasting media, stymied his legislative proposals. The Parliament refused to pass important reform legislation and Khatami's
loyalty to the Leader and to an Islamic form of government limited
the actions he was prepared to take. After the government brutally
put down major riots in Tehran in July 1999, the president began to
lose his appetite for reform. The judiciary closed over 200 reformist
publications and jailed or sidelined many reformist clerics close to
the president. A sense of disillusionment and cynicism set in with
the reformers.

Ahmadinejad's presidency

The victory of Ahmadinejad, who had been given no chance of
winning, completed the capture by conservatives of all branches of
government. He is the son of a blacksmith who grew up in a religious
family near Tehran, was active in the anti-shah movement and later
served in the Basij (Islamic militia) and, during the war with Iraq, the
Revolutionary Guard. He received a doctorate in traffic engineering,
and in 2003 was appointed mayor of Tehran.

Why was he elected? After eight years of lofty dialogue from the
reformers about Islam and democracy, many Iranians were more
concerned about their difficult economic situation. Ahmadinejad
presented himself as a man of the people, one who preferred a simple
lifestyle and was not associated with the corruption of the ruling

Iranian President Mahmoud Ahmadinejad at the Conference on Interaction and Confidence Building Measures in Asia (CICA) in Istanbul in 2010.

establishment. He geared his appeal to the poor, who were concerned about unemployment and inflation, and promised to share with them Iran's oil bounty. This appeal resonated with the voters, who widely distrusted Ali-Akbar Hashemi-Rafsanjani, his opponent in the runoff, and regarded him as corrupt.

Ahmadinejad's advent represents the coming to power of a new generation whose worldview was formed by the war with Iraq. This group, now in its fifties, is replacing the cohort in their seventies like Rafsanjani, Khamenei, Mehdi Karroubi and Mir-Hossein Mousavi that made the revolution. Although a minority, they are determined to keep alive the ideals of the revolution, and their policies aim to take Iran back to an era that most Iranians never knew or from which they have moved on. They are more religious and from poorer, more rural and military backgrounds. Many prominent reformers who also fought against Iraq, however, are unhappy about those who constantly invoke the war to

89

justify repressive policies. Key wartime decisions—such as when to end the war—have now become contested political issues.

Ahmadinejad has often been in conflict with the conservative Parliament, partly because of his appointment of cronies and unqualified people and his refusal to implement legislation. His resistance to consult or compromise with others, his populist rhetoric and squandering of windfall oil revenues has led to widespread consternation. He has not seriously cracked down on corruption, as it would quickly lead to conflict with many entrenched interests, including members of the clerical establishment. Ahmadinejad's strident rhetoric against Israel, denigration of the Holocaust as "a lie" and belligerent pursuit of a nuclear program have led to international ostracism. His proposed policies have been routinely challenged by other conservatives. The relationship between Ahmadinejad and Khamenei was badly strained in April 2011 when, in a direct challenge to the Leader, the president attempted to fire the intelligence minister.

Many of Ahmadinejad's appointments come from the Basij or the Revolutionary Guard, and their role in the government has now eclipsed that of the ulama. Since he was first elected, Ahmadinejad has worked assiduously to place thousands of his partisans in positions throughout the government. However, in the current conflict, the Revolutionary Guard has backed Khamenei, not Ahmadinejad. The Revolutionary Guard also plays a major, if often unscrutinized, role in the economy. Its engineering arm, Khatam al-Anbiya, has a role in many major infrastructural projects, such as roads, bridges, highways, dams and ports, as well as prestige projects such as the new Tehran metro and an oil pipeline to Pakistan.

The Green Movement: over already?

The ruthlessness of the security services, and their loyalty to Khamenei and Ahmadinejad, was starkly demonstrated by their harsh crackdown on the opposition "Green Movement" that arose after the fraudulent presidential elections in June 2009. Ahmadinejad was declared the winner almost immediately, amid what seemed to be large-scale vote rigging, as massive street protests involving millions of people broke out in Tehran and other cities. Despite a media blackout, the brutal crackdown on largely peaceful protesters was revealed to the world by participants themselves using new technologies such as cell phones and social networking sites like Facebook and Twitter. (Between June 7 and 26, there were over 2 million tweets about the election by half a million users. It later transpired that many of these came from outside Iran, but they nevertheless attracted worldwide publicity to the cause.) The murder of one young protester (or observer), Neda Agha-Sultan, on June 20 was caught on video and widely replayed, and her photo became an icon of the resistance.

These antigovernment protests were unprecedented since the 1979 revolution itself. The indifference and apathy that had characterized post-Khatami politics were gone, and new slogans, such as "Death to

Demonstrators hold a silent vigil on July 30, 2009, to mark the 40th day since the death of Neda Agha-Sultan, a young woman who was killed during post-election protests in Tehran. Her death became an international rallying cry.

the Dictator" (referring to Khamenei) breached longstanding redlines. When forced off the streets, many shouted "Allahu Akbar" (God is Great) from the rooftops at night, mimicking a tactic used during the revolution. On August 13, the government acknowledged having detained 4,000 people because of the protests, and many were forced to undergo show trials. A report by Human Rights Watch released in February 2010 documented that since the elections there had been "repeated serious human rights abuses that include extra-judicial killings, violations of the rights to freedom of assembly and expression, and the prohibition of torture, not to mention arbitrary arrest and detention and countless due process violations."

The losing presidential candidates, Mousavi and Karroubi, along with former President Khatami, were the symbolic leaders of the protest, but were not directing it. In the months after the election a split between these old guard figures and the youthful protesters became increasingly clear. The original aim of the opposition was to have an honest recount of the vote. In light of the harsh crackdown and the Ahmadinejad clique's increasing consolidation of power in its own hands, however, demands were increasingly voiced for a complete overhaul of the political system, with an emphasis on the republican rather than the Islamic part. This was farther than the opposition's titular heads, who were loyal to the Leader and still supported the political system set up three decades ago, were prepared to go.

The legitimacy of the government, and Ayatollah Khamenei, was seriously tarnished by these events. As Ayatollah Montazeri, probably the most respected cleric in Iran at the time, said, "They should at least have the courage to declare that this government is neither a republic nor Islamic, with nobody allowed to protest, comment or criticize." Major street protests petered out in the face of the brutal crackdown, but the anger and resentment among people simmered under the surface. Protesters took advantage of days favored by the regime to celebrate Islamic or revolutionary events to stage their own gatherings.

Convinced that outside enemies were waging a "soft war" against it, the government kept up its cultural offensive and tried to control the media and purge universities of any students or faculty deemed disloyal. In October 2010, it announced a major effort to revamp the curriculum and remove any Western content (such as in social sciences or the humanities) in the name of Islamization. Ahmadinejad continued to consolidate power by seeking to sideline traditional conservatives who opposed him, such as Rafsanjani. A massive brain drain continues, as Iranian scholars and professionals seek refuge abroad. The manipulation of the media and human rights abuses continue apace. More Iranian journalists had fled into exile than from any other country, the Committee to Protect Journalists reported in June 2010.

So far no new leadership of the protest movement has appeared, and many members are in jail. Many feared the Green Movement was over, although major protests broke out again on February 14, 2011, in solidarity with the Egyptian revolution. However, these were suppressed and Mousavi and Karroubi were put under house arrest. Could the opposition be reinvigorated? It would need to develop a wider base of support, notably among the working class and bazaar (merchant class) and those working in the oil fields. Faezeh Hashemi-Rafsanjani, the outpoken daughter of the former president, complained in September 2010, "Presently, everything is upside down, wrong is right, the unjust pretend to be unjustly treated, those who aim to destroy the country and the religion call themselves servants of the nation. Imbeciles are at the top, and managers and the distinguished are in prison, or have been dismissed, or have had to flee the country. All of this would be painful for any Iranian who has a modicum of pride."

The current economy

One of the main reasons that Ahmadinejad has felt free to indulge in bluster and spend money recklessly is that the price of oil, the source of 83% of Iran's export revenues, has been high since he has been in office. Iran has the world's third-largest oil reserves and second-largest gas reserves, but due to a lack of investment production is less now than at the time of the revolution. It is now about

93

3.7mmb/d, with consumption running at 2.1 mmb/d. The oil ministry warned in June 2011 that if needed investment is not forthcoming, by 2015 output could drop to 2.7 mmb/d, leaving little for export.

The key issues today are the lack of jobs (especially for the youth and well-educated), delayed payment of wages and poor standard of living. Of the almost 1 million people entering the job market annually, only half find work. Iran's 12-month inflation rate (put at 17.5% in August 2011 by the Central Bank of Iran) and a lack of foreign investment are souring hope for the future. Corruption is regarded as worse than at the time of the shah.

Serious reforms are needed in Iran's economic structure, including less state regulation and greater privatization. Foundations, or *bonyads*, control a major part of the economy and are regarded as inefficient and corrupt. They are under the control of the Leader and are not subject to scrutiny by Parliament or the government. The widespread intervention of the Revolutionary Guard and Basij in the economy is hampering the private sector and even challenging the bonyads.

Subsidies to help the poor pay for staples such as fuel, bread, rice, sugar, cooking oil, cheese and prescription drugs, and the provision below cost of water, power, telephone and urban transport, by 2010 were estimated to cost the government between $70 billion and $100 billion a year. One of Ahmadinejad's priorities is to phase out such subsidies over five years, with the first stage implemented in December 2010. Iranians are profligate users of gasoline, which until then only cost 40 cents a gallon. (Private individuals now pay $1.60 a gallon for their quota of 16 gallons; beyond this they can buy all they can afford at $2.80 a gallon.) In lieu of subsidies, people receive a monthly payment of about $40. The subsidy reform program has so far been regarded as a success and has not led to protests, although inflation and rising unemployment is a concern for the future.

Sanctions

So far four rounds of UN sanctions (the first passed by the Security Council in December 2006 and the latest in June 2010) have been imposed to force Iran to suspend its nuclear program. These restrictions, along with unilateral U.S. sanctions against trade and investment in Iran imposed in 1995 and strengthened in 1996, have increasingly cut off Iran from the world economy and banking system. In addition, European Union (EU) governments have instituted measures targeting Iranian finance, banking, insurance, transportation and energy. These have caused companies to refrain from investing in Iranian energy projects lest the U.S. retaliate (by way of "secondary sanctions") against any firms operating there. (Due to lack of refinery capacity, until recently Iran was importing 40% of its gasoline.) Although Tehran announced in September 2010 that it had achieved self-sufficiency in imports, this is doubtful and in June 2011 *International Oil Daily* estimated that imports accounted for 15% of usage. Iran, however, has reduced gasoline imports significantly by reducing consumption and curtailing smuggling. In May 2011, Obama implemented the Comprehensive Iran Sanctions, Accountability and Divestment Act of 2010, which amends the Iran Sanctions Act and for the first time calls for sanctions targeting Iran's gasoline imports.

Youth culture

The Iran of today is much different from the time of the shah, when rapid modernization and the rejection by some of imposed Westernization led to serious social strains. A majority of Iranians have grown up with no memory of the shah or life under a secular government. The revolution brought the age of mass politics to Iran, and left Iranians—especially women—with the conviction that they were entitled to participate in the political process. Women were in the forefront during the 2009 protests.

Around 60% of the population is now below the age of 30, and demographic patterns have changed significantly. Rapidly declining fertility rates and later marriage have slowed population growth and will lead to social consequences in the future. The very high birthrate of 6.5 to 7 children per woman maintained from 1950 to 1980 then dropped precipitously, and 2010 figures suggest the natural rate of increase is just 1.3%. Late marriage (in 2004, the average age of marriage for men was 27.7 and for women, 23.9, with higher and

**Young Iranian women studying graphics software
at Dibagaran Tehran, a private IT university in Tehran, Iran, in 2010.**

disputed figures released in 2009) is reportedly fostering a sexual revolution. The divorce rate is soaring as women seek to escape unhappy marriages. There is increasing gender equality (60% of university students are women, and it appears the government may now institute quotas to reduce this number). Women in Iran play a much larger public role than in other Persian Gulf states.

An important theme of the revolution was the emphasis on Islam's role in resisting the Western cultural onslaught and restoring moral order. This led to the government's insistence that women cover their hair and bodies, and segregation of the sexes increased, for example, on buses. This has led to a never-ending struggle between women and state enforcers who seek to guard against "bad hijab," particularly in large urban areas.

In an information age, young Iranians are much better informed than before about the outside world, and the internet has achieved huge popularity. Iran has the highest number of computer users in the Middle East, and in 2006 was estimated to have between 70,000 and 100,000 blogs. Young Iranians' expertise with the internet came in handy at the time of the upheaval in the summer of 2009, when they outfoxed the government's attempts at censorship.

The Islamic government can claim many achievements. Prof. Ervand Abrahamian, a leading historian of Iran, suggests that it has survived for three decades because of its emphasis on populism and commitment to improving the lot of the poor by creating a welfare state and giving priority to social over military expenditure. Since the 1970s, the rate of infant mortality has dropped, while life expectancy and literacy rates have gone up significantly (the rate of illiteracy has been reduced from 53% to 15% since the revolution). Roads, safe water and communications have been extended throughout the countryside, and the historic divide between the city and countryside has been greatly reduced.

The downside of the revolution, however, is also apparent. Only one fifth of high school students pass college entrance exams, and only 5% go to prestigious institutions like the University of Tehran. The country is 72% urban (as opposed to half at the time of the revolution), where the lack of jobs, housing and entertainment has led to serious discontent. There is a strong link between unemployment and drug addiction that is taking a serious toll on society. Iran has the highest proportion of opium users of any country in the world, according to the UN, and heroin is making inroads among the youth. The human rights situation is dismal, and Sunni Muslims, as well as minority religious groups such as Christians, Jews and Bahais, may be subject to restrictions or harassment.

Evolving foreign policy

Iran's foreign policy goal since the revolution has been to assert its independence of external powers, especially the U.S. It has aimed to counteract economic sanctions by cultivating better ties with non-European states such as India, Russia and China. It has also been supportive of political factions that oppose Israel, such as the Pal-

Iran: Land of the Lion and the Sun

IRAN, WHICH MEANS "the land of the Aryans," claims a tradition of kingship reaching back 2,500 years. Like Iraq, Iran was conquered by Arab Muslim invaders in the 7th century A.D. It was later an important part of the Abbasid Empire, centered in Baghdad. Iran was subject to a series of invasions by Turkic (non-Persian) peoples from Central Asia from the 11th to the 15th centuries, and was ruled almost continuously by leaders of Turkish origin until 1925. Iran was never colonized by a European power, and the constant goal of Iranian foreign policy has been to maintain the country's independence.

The Pahlavi dynasty of Reza Shah (1925–41) and his son, Mohammad Reza (1941–79), tried to create a modern, secular state and promoted a strong Iranian nationalism. Both were authoritarian rulers, identified with the military, and were strongly anti-Communist. They did not tolerate internal dissent. Mohammad Reza Shah Pahlavi was known for his friendship with the U.S., which helped return him to the throne in 1953 after he briefly fled the country during the oil nationalization crisis. The shah's close ties to the U.S. became one of his main liabilities at the time of the revolution.

Pahlavi rule was brought down in January 1979 by a coalition of religious groups, middle class merchants *(bazaaris)*, and liberal reformist and leftist groups. Leadership of the country was then assumed by the ulama, under

estinian group Hamas in Gaza and Hezbollah, the Shi'i militia in Lebanon. Iran also has carved out spheres of influence in eastern Afghanistan around the city of Herat, in Lebanon, and in southern Iraq. Under Ahmadinejad, Tehran has cultivated the Arab "street" and played on anger toward the U.S. and Israel. However, it is clear from the WikiLeaks documents that there is a lot of suspicion and hostility toward Iran on the part of Arab states. A poll released in July 2011 by the Arab American Institute in Washington shows that approval of Iran's role in the region has plummeted. According to the institutes's founder and president, James Zogby, "In the face of all the direction of Ayatollah Ruhollah Khomeini (1902–89). The monarchy was abolished and the country became an Islamic Republic in April 1979. Since that time clerical factions have sharply debated issues such as the course of Iran's foreign relations (including the export of revolution and whether to resume ties to the U.S.), state control versus privatization of the economy, land reform and the proper role of women.

The leader and successor to Khomeini is Ali Khamenei (b. 1939) who served as president from 1981 to 1989 and is regarded as more of a political figure than a religious scholar. He long ruled in collaboration, and sometimes rivalry, with Ali-Akbar Hashemi-Rafsanjani (b. 1934), who served as president from 1989 to 1997. Rafsanjani, regarded as a pragmatist and canny politician, was chairman of the Assembly of Experts (2007–11), which chooses the Leader, and he still chairs the Expediency Council, which resolves stalemates between Parliament and the Council of Guardians. He broke with Khamenei over the Green Movement protests and, while currently sidelined, is a survivor who remains a key regime insider.

Iran today is an ethnically diverse nation of some 78 million people. The principal groups are Persians, Turks, Kurds and Arabs. There are no reliable figures on the religious breakdown, but Shi'is constitute the vast majority of the population, with Sunnis (especially tribal peoples who live in border areas) the largest minority. There are a small number of non-Muslims, including Bahais, Christians, Jews and Zoroastrians. ※

this, Iran's behaviour is seen by Arab public opinion not as a counter to America's hostile domination, but as [a] source of instability seeking to exploit troubled areas for its own gain."

One important difference is that foreign policy is no longer made by one man, but rather is the product of contending factions in Tehran. This has resulted, especially in the early years, in a lack of consistency that led to Arab unease about Iranian intentions. The battle between the "idealists" and "realists" led initially to the ascendancy of the former, who placed an emphasis on Islam over Iranian nationalism and sought to export the revolution. However, a more pragmatic approach eventually prevailed, and in the 1980s and 1990s, under the Rafsanjani and then Khatami administrations, Iran vigorously pursued détente and confidence-building measures in the Gulf. As the revolutionary idealism of the early years waned, a less confrontational style developed. By the mid-1980s, Iranian rhetoric had cooled and Iran sought better relations with other states, including its Gulf neighbors.

The two military campaigns waged by the Bush II Administration, the first in 2001 to liberate Afghanistan and the second in 2003 to liberate Iraq, have significantly enhanced Iran's standing in the region by neutralizing longtime foes. However, Iran now finds itself surrounded on all sides by U.S.-backed states (including Iraq, Afghanistan, Pakistan and the GCC), which makes it feel extremely vulnerable. Should the Assad government in Syria fall, Iran would lose a longtime source of support and a conduit for sending arms to Hezbollah in Lebanon. The reality is that Iran can do little to counter U.S. military domination of the Gulf except argue, as had the shah, that foreign forces should be withdrawn and security left to the littoral states.

The era of good feeling that prevailed under President Khatami's "dialogue among civilizations" has now evaporated as the policies of the Ahmadinejad government, and its growing emphasis on threats and regime security, have forced Gulf Arab states on the defensive. Accusations of Iranian meddling in Bahrain have now poisoned the atmosphere. The increased role for the Revolutionary Guard in domestic and foreign policy at the expense of the foreign ministry is very unsettling. Determining Iran's intentions in the Persian Gulf poses a major dilemma for regional states and the international community. Iran's rightful predominance there looms large in the historical memory of Iranians, although control was always episodic and not continuous. The Islamic Republic, while adding a new religious dimension to Iran's foreign policy, has continued to observe some well-established principles. These include the conviction that Iran ought to be the preeminent power in the Gulf, that Iran is entitled to control Abu Musa and the Tunb islands by historic right, and that external powers should leave the Gulf. Iran, however, has been cautious to maintain correct relations there. In the case of Dubai, for instance, which has helped Iran evade sanctions, there is a strong economic incentive not to let the dispute over the islands derail major trade and banking ties.

Over the past few years there have been a number of troubling incidents in the Persian Gulf, including the capture and detention of British sailors in the Shatt al-Arab who supposedly strayed into Iranian territorial waters in June 2004 and March 2007. These incidents highlight the need to have clearly agreed-upon international boundaries. Particularly galling are renewed questions Iran has raised about the leadership of the Gulf monarchies. Periodic suggestions that the Gulf rulers lack legitimacy seem a throwback to 30 years ago when Iran sought to export its revolution to the region. Saudi Arabia and Bahrain have long been concerned that Iran would activate disgruntled Shi'i groups to promote its causes and see Bahrain as proof of this. Iranian officials and journalists have periodically recalled Iranian control over Bahrain—where the Persian presence was driven out in 1783—and implied that Bahrain rightfully belongs to

BEHROUZ MEHRI/AFP/GETTY IMAGES

Leading opposition leaders in Iran, l. to r.: defeated Iranian presidential candidate Mir-Hossein Mousavi, defeated reformist presidential candidate Mehdi Karroubi and Iran's former reformist president Mohammad Khatami.

101

it. This has led to widespread Arab anger and apprehension. Tehran's major objective, first broached at the end of the second Persian Gulf war, is a nonaggression treaty of the Gulf states. Tehran frequently has asserted its view that the littoral states themselves should assume prime responsibility for Gulf security. However, the GCC states are not ready to sign on. Without a hostile Iraq to serve as a counterweight to Iran, they are driven closer to the Western embrace.

Iran's intentions in Iraq are of prime concern to the U.S., for Iran is in a position, should it choose, to greatly increase instability in Iraq and complicate the U.S. troop withdrawal. In July 2011, the U.S. ramped up criticism that Iran was supplying weapons to Iraqi insurgents. This accusation has been questioned by critics, who demand more evidence. (For example, in light of similar charges a military task force that examined the data for 2008 found that few Iranian weapons had been confiscated, according to investigative reporter Gareth Porter.) Iran's interests are numerous. One is religious: two of the holiest cities for Shi'i Muslims, Najaf and Karbala, are located there, and since early Islamic times Iranian pilgrims have visited them. The Shi'i seminaries in Najaf were the main center for the faith until the rise of rival Qom in Iran in the 20th century, and since the fall of Saddam there has been an increased flow of Iranian pilgrims. The most senior Shi'i religious leader in Iraq, Ayatollah Sistani, is of Iranian origin and has good ties with Iran, as do many government figures.

Also, there are security concerns. Iranians' experience of war has left them determined that Iraq should never be allowed to threaten them again. One irritant is the Kurdish rebel group Party of Free Life of Kurdistan (PJAK), whose bases in northern Iraq Iran is accused of shelling on and off for the past five years, with an escalation of the conflict in July 2011. There is the issue of Iraqi reparations for damage done to Iran. A peace treaty still has not been concluded, and Iraq has not reaffirmed the validity of the border agreement along the Shatt al-Arab river that was reached between the two states in 1975.

Iran wants to preserve Iraq's territorial integrity, prevent the emergence of an independent Kurdistan (lest it serve as an inspiration to Iranian Kurds), ensure the continuation of a Shi'i-dominated government in Baghdad and, to the degree possible, reduce U.S. influence there. Iran understands, however, that Iraq still needs American assistance in many areas, including security training. Tehran's ability to influence its protégés in Iraq may be at its apogee, as Iraqi nationalism increasingly comes to the fore and Sunni and secular forces resume a more prominent role.

Iran has many levers of power in Iraq, and permeable borders permit easy movement. There are many people of Persian heritage living there, and since 2003 Shi'i pilgrims have flooded the holy cities. In the extended struggle to form a new Iraqi government in 2010, all the major players sought Iranian advice and the Iranian candidate is reckoned to have won. The Revolutionary Guard (especially their external arm, the Quds Force) has been regularly accused by the U.S. of stoking the insurgency, but definitive proof has been lacking. All such factors serve Iran's interest in shaping an Iraq that will be friendly but not threatening, and ensuring that internal unrest does not get out of control. In Iraq, Iran is succeeding by playing a waiting game.

Iran's relations with the U.S.

This has been one of the most sensitive issues and one on which the Iranian leadership is divided. The election of Ahmadinejad quickly cooled the warmer ties that had been developing under President Khatami. The presence of U.S. forces in the Persian Gulf is a major irritant, as is the U.S. trade embargo and its worldwide efforts to isolate Iran from the world economy. Iran also demands the return of financial assets frozen long ago by the American government (the claim is for $20 billion to $30 billion). Iran would like to have Iraq hand over members of the Mujahideen, an opposition group detained in Iraq that both the U.S. and Iran regard as terrorists. So far the U.S. has waffled on the issue, evidently because some regard the members as intelligence assets. In 2003, Tehran showed an interest in striking a "grand bargain" with the U.S. to resolve outstanding issues, but the Bush Administration declined the offer. Above all, Iran says it wants to be treated respectfully. (Following the unproductive talks in early 2011, Western powers rebuffed a renewed offer to talk in May 2011 as not serious.) There is some question whether the Iranian government is really prepared or able to negotiate right now.

The nuclear issue

The issue that arouses the most international concern is Iran's nuclear program. The U.S. and many other countries suspect that the civilian nuclear infrastructure that Iran is developing could be accompanied by or diverted into a clandestine weapons program. These suspicions have been fueled by accusations by the International Atomic Energy Agency (IAEA) of a long-standing pattern

ATTA KENARE/AFP/GETTY IMAGES

The reactor building at the Russian-built Bushire nuclear power plant in southern Iran on August 21, 2010, during a ceremony initiating the transfer of Russia-supplied fuel to the facility after more than three decades of delay.

of noncompliance with Iran's obligations to report all its nuclear activities and sites. These include an underground enrichment plant at Natanz, a heavy water plant at Arak, and an enrichment plant at Fordo, near Qom. Belated revelations about the program have created a crisis of confidence between Iran and the rest of the world. Yukiya Amano, director general of IAEA, said on June 6, 2011, that the agency had "information related to possible past or current undisclosed nuclear-related activities that seem to point to the existence of possible military dimensions to Iran's nuclear programme."

Iran, for its part, insists that its aims are wholly peaceful, that as a signer of the 1968 Nuclear Non-Proliferation Treaty (NPT) it has the right to nuclear energy and that it has cooperated with the IAEA to permit on-site monitoring. Iran maintains that the U.S. seeks to deny its legitimate right to such technology because it is fundamentally opposed to the Islamic Republic. Iran insists on its right to possess a complete nuclear fuel cycle, including indigenous conversion and enrichment facilities. Iran claims that it does not intend to make weapons and that doing so has been expressly forbidden by a fatwa by Ayatollah Khamenei.

In October 2010 Iran started loading fuel rods in its nuclear power plant at Bushire on the Persian Gulf, but in a major unexplained setback (probably due in part to damage caused by the Stuxnet computer virus) they had to be removed the following February. The plant finally went online in May 2011 and in September was connected to the country's electricity grid. The U.S. does not regard Bushire as a proliferation risk, as all fuel will be supplied and removed by Russia, and the plant will be under IAEA monitoring.

Why is Iran pursuing a nuclear program in the first place? Although some have questioned why a country with rich oil and gas resources would need nuclear energy, there is an economic rationale. Iran is faced with a large population that has doubled since the time of the revolution. Production of oil is declining due to lack of maintenance of the oil fields and an inability to obtain spare parts. At the expected rate of use, Iran could be a net importer of petroleum within a decade.

One reason that Iran might want to move to a nuclear deterrent is to assure its security without depending on anyone else. Iranians remember the Iran-Iraq War, when an unprovoked Iraqi attack was not condemned by the UN or other states, and Saddam's government unleashed chemical weapons on Iranian troops with impunity. Iranians feel vulnerable and alone, and in a neighborhood with nuclear-armed states such as Israel, Pakistan and India, Iran may feel that it must match their power. Iranians may have drawn the conclusion that the U.S. did not hesitate to attack Iraq because it was not a nuclear state, but has refrained from attacking North Korea because it is. A bomb, therefore, would be the best insurance against "regime change."

Efforts by the EU led in November 2004 to an agreement that Iran would temporarily suspend all conversion and enrichment activities in order to build confidence about its intentions. Iran canceled this agreement in August 2005 after it concluded it would not receive an acceptable offer from the Europeans. In June 2008, the foreign ministers of Britain, the U.S., China, France, Germany and Russia made a generous offer to help Iran develop a modern nuclear energy program with a guaranteed fuel supply. This repeated and expanded upon an earlier offer of June 2006. Because of the condition that Iran suspend enrichment and reprocessing, Iran declined. A proposal by the U.S., France and Russia in the fall of 2009 that Iran swap some of its low-enriched uranium (LEU) in return for fuel rods it could use in a medical reactor was revived in May 2010 by Brazil and Turkey and accepted by Iran. However, this was not implemented and Iran has now lost interest. Further talks in Geneva, Switzerland, in December 2010 and Istanbul, Turkey, in January 2011 were not fruitful. Iran did not seem prepared to negotiate seriously and no date has been set for further talks. Many suspect that Iran is playing for time by seeking to drag out the negotiations. A proposal by Russia in July 2011 to restart "step-by-step" negotiations was welcomed by Iran, but seems unlikely to gain traction.

Estimates about the critical issue of how long it would take for Iran to master the technology needed to build a bomb have been revised repeatedly over the years. The outgoing head of Mossad, the Israeli intelligence agency, said in January 2011 that Iran would not have a nuclear capability before 2015, and the International Institute for Strategic Studies estimated in February 2011 that it would take Iran at least two years to make a weapon. By the summer of 2010, it was clear that that progress had slowed, perhaps due to technical difficulties caused by the Stuxnet virus. Any move to convert its stock of LEU to weapons-grade material, known as "breakout," would quickly be detected by IAEA observers. (By September 2011 Iran had on hand about 4,500 kilograms of LEU—enough, after enrichment, for four bombs.)

So far the IAEA has not found definitive evidence that Iran is pursuing nuclear weapons, and Ahmadinejad insists that "the nuclear file is closed." Despite years of on-again, off-again talks, Iran has shown no indication that it is willing to compromise on enrichment, which the U.S. regards as a redline. As Prof. Farideh Farhi of the University of Hawaii notes, constant conflicts between the executive and legislative branches have hindered the decisionmaking process.

Prospects

By fall 2011, the political situation in Iran was still very unsettled, and the Arab Spring did not appear to have much effect in reinvigorating the opposition. Politically, sights are set on parliamentary elections in March 2012 and presidential elections in 2013, although it is uncertain if reformers will be able and willing to participate.

Clearly the government and Leader suffered a serious loss of legitimacy in the wake of the 2009 elections. Political infighting continues among the conservatives, as they increasingly aggregate all power to themselves. The opposition, while cowed, is resentful and angry, although not ready to carry out another revolution. Ahmadinejad, while now a lame duck, has some support and could serve out the remainder of his term (which expires in 2013) as long as he retains the support of Khamenei. Iran is a country where there are many centers of power and vested interests that can obstruct his policies. As noted by Iran analyst Ray Takeyh, the Islamic Republic has reached an impasse: "It can neither appease the opposition nor forcibly repress it out of existence."

In part to elicit domestic support, the government has emphasized the foreign threat and is obsessed with the idea that enemies are trying to foment a "velvet revolution" against it. "Khamenei knows that enmity toward the U.S. is an important pillar of the 1979 revolution for hard-liners, and has become central to the identity of the Islamic Republic," according to CEIP analyst Karim Sadjadpour. Even should Ahmadinejad be replaced, it would likely be by another conservative and so major policies might not change.

One unknown factor is the longevity of Khamenei. When he dies, the question of the role of the *faqih* (Islamic jurist) will again come to the fore, and could be addressed by an amendment to the constitution diminishing or abolishing the position. The increased prominence of military and security elements in running the state points to a continued reduction of the role of the ulama, although they are still needed to bestow legitimacy. However, the Revolutionary Guard may be divided. Reportedly many voted for Khatami, and Ahmadinejad may be unsure of their continued allegiance to him.

The contrast between the narrow group of old men and ideologues who currently run the state and its youthful population could not be greater. The hope of Iran is its young people, who are thoroughly disillusioned with decades of Islamic government. They make up the vast majority and, because of the internet, are well aware of what they are missing. The protests of 2009 were a major milestone for the Iranian Republic, and their aftermath will take a long time to process. As suggested by sociologist Said Amir Arjomand, Iran's Islamic revolution has not ended, and the construction of a new political order is a long-term process.

6

U.S. Policy: Retrospect and Prospects

THE U.S. IS A RELATIVE LATECOMER to the Middle East and especially the Persian Gulf. After World War II, it became the dominant external power in Iran and Saudi Arabia, as the Soviets gained influence in Iraq. Britain remained the protector of the smaller Arab states in the Gulf and the main naval power there until 1971, when it voluntarily withdrew. Afterward, the U.S. counted on the "twin pillars" of Iran and Saudi Arabia to keep the oil flowing and oppose possible Soviet inroads. The twin-pillars policy fitted in with the Nixon Doctrine, announced in July 1969, which called for regional powers to take on greater responsibility for collective security. This policy began unraveling in 1978 as the Iranian revolution gained momentum. Thereafter, a power vacuum developed in the Gulf.

The fall of the shah in January 1979 was one in a string of events in the Middle East that adversely affected U.S. interests and led Washington to take a more assertive military role. The shah's exit was followed by the taking of American hostages in Iran in November 1979 and the onset of the Iran-Iraq War in September 1980. Moreover, there were internal challenges by fundamentalist Muslim groups to governments friendly to the U.S. The Great Mosque in Mecca was occupied in November 1979, and Egyptian President Anwar Sadat was assassinated in October 1981.

The Carter Administration (1977–81) came to regard the region extending from Egypt to Pakistan as a "crescent of crisis." In January 1980, following the Soviet invasion of Afghanistan, the American President proclaimed what became known as the Carter Doctrine. He said, in a warning to the Soviets, that "an attempt by any outside force to gain control of the Persian Gulf region...will be repelled by any means necessary, including military force." This declaration was followed by

Americans and Iranians: Strained Encounters

SINCE THE IRANIAN REVOLUTION, relations between Washington and Tehran have been characterized by mutual hostility and aborted attempts at reconciliation. This has arisen out of policy differences and, behind that, mutual misperceptions that have left each nation with sharply differing historical memories of the other.

Americans had little contact with Iran before World War II, when 30,000 U.S. troops were sent there to help secure a supply line to Russia. After the war, Washington backed Iran's demand that Soviet troops be withdrawn from the northwestern Iranian province of Azerbaijan. When the Soviets retreated, Iran looked on the U.S. as a protector. The young shah, Mohammad Reza Pahlavi, sought U.S. military and economic assistance, and the CIA helped restore him to power after he was briefly forced out of the country in 1953. Over the next quarter century (1953–79), Washington developed a close relationship with the Pahlavis, who turned Iran into an anti-Communist bulwark and became good customers for U.S. arms.

The shah was regarded by most Americans as a modernizer who continued the work of his father, Reza Shah, of centralizing power, strengthening the military and building a secular state. He also guaranteed the security of the Gulf in the wake of the British withdrawal. In 1978, some 50,000 Americans were living and working in Iran, and between 1962 and 1976 the creation of the U.S. Rapid Deployment Force (later renamed the Central Command), to be sent if necessary to the Gulf region. These developments "marked a major threshold in the evolution of U.S. strategy and a new conviction that this region represented a major strategic zone of U.S. vital interests, demanding both sustained attention at the highest levels of U.S. policymaking and direct U.S. engagement in support of specifically U.S. interests," according to Gary Sick, executive director of the Gulf/2000 Project at Columbia University.

When military force was introduced, however, it was used not against an external power but a regional one. It became clear to the Reagan Administration (1981–89) that the major threat to stability did not come from the Soviet Union but from the military confrontation between Iran and Iraq. In policy statements under both the

---

almost 1,800 U.S. Peace Corps volunteers served there. Iran, as President Carter declared in a New Year's eve toast in Tehran on December 31, 1977, appeared to be "an island of stability in one of the more troubled areas of the world." How could he, and America, have gotten it so wrong?

The Iranian version

The Iranian encounter with the U.S. is a story of disillusionment and betrayal. For the first half of the 20th century, Iranian impressions of America, limited though they were, had been positive. Unlike European imperial powers such as Britain and Russia, who had long interfered in Iranian affairs, the U.S. was regarded as a disinterested observer with no designs on Iranian territory. Iranians assumed that because of its democratic ideals, the U.S. would support Iran's nationalization of its major resource, oil, during the early 1950s. Many were bitterly disappointed when the U.S. instead backed its ally, Britain, in the dispute, and intervened in Iranian affairs, first by helping to depose the popular nationalist leader Mohammad Mossadeq in 1953 and then helping maintain an autocratic shah in power for the next 25 years.

When President Carter was asked about this in 1980 he referred to it as "ancient history." Yet many Iranians have not forgotten, for they believe that these actions cut short Iran's last chance for democracy. In a CNN interview in 1988, former President Khatami denounced Washington's

Carter and Reagan Administrations, the U.S. declared itself neutral, supported the territorial integrity and political independence of both countries, endorsed mediation efforts, and announced it would not sell weapons to either side. (In reality, following Iranian successes on the battlefield, U.S. policy began a tilt toward Iraq by the fall of 1983, and in 1985–86 the Reagan Administration secretly sold arms to Iran in what became known as the Iran-Contra scandal.) With the introduction of an American armada in 1987 to protect shipping, the U.S. became fully committed to the defense of the Gulf and the days of operating "over the horizon" were over.

After the Iraqi occupation of Kuwait in August 1990, Bush I

"flawed policy of domination" of Iran, specifically mentioning the 1953 coup. Many regarded the shah as a creature of the Americans, who shared blame for his increasingly autocratic ways, the human rights abuses of his secret police, SAVAK, and his coddling of the military. His willingness to

BETTMANN/CORBIS

U.S. President Jimmy Carter and Shah Mohammad Reza Pahlavi of Iran toast following a dinner in Niavaran Palace in Tehran, Iran, December 31, 1977.

vowed to liberate Kuwait and assembled an international alliance under UN auspices to do so. He declared that the independence of Saudi Arabia was "of vital interest" to the U.S. and drew "a line in the sand" to protect it. If Saddam had seized Saudi Arabia, he would have controlled over 40% of the world's oil supplies and had a stranglehold on the world's economy. Oil, indeed, was a major reason for the unprecedented U.S. commitment. "Laid bare, American policy in the Gulf comes down to this: troops have been sent to retain control of oil in the hands of a pro-American Saudi Arabia, so prices will remain low," wrote Thomas L. Friedman, then a diplomatic correspondent for *The New York Times*. With the approval

---

deal with Israel and supply it with oil was also at issue. For a large segment of the popular classes who were bypassed on the road to prosperity, the shah's Westernization efforts and his contempt for the ulama fueled resentment. They regarded the ulama as the preservers of Iranian cultural identity and accepted Ayatollah Khomeini as their leader. Eventually, they joined with others, some secular, to make the revolution.

On the eve of revolution in the late 1970s, the U.S. government was unaware of the strength of domestic opposition in Iran, had virtually no contacts with the ulama, and continued to back the shah until almost the bitter end. Many Iranians were surprised by America's hostility to their revolution, and relations were strained to the breaking point during the hostage crisis (November 1979–January 1981). Since then, the U.S. image of Iran has been one of demonstrators shouting "death to America" and turbaned ayatollahs denouncing the U.S. as the "Great Satan." But Americans' image of Iran is now seriously out of date, and Iranians won new respect for their antigovernment uprising in 2009.

Iranians, it has been said, are the most pro-American people in the Middle East, although their government is the most anti-American—just the opposite of the situation prevailing in Arab countries. After 9/11, candlelight vigils were held in sympathy in Tehran. Because many young Iranians are heavy internet users they are familiar with American films and popular culture. Many Iranians took refuge in the U.S. after the revolution and maintain close connections with families back home. Official U.S. statements emphasize that policymakers have a problem only with Tehran's policies. 🌸

of Congress, an allied air assault on Iraq began in January 1991, followed the next month by a 100-hour ground campaign, Desert Storm, which led to a rapid Iraqi surrender. The wartime coalition, however, did not long hold together.

From war to war

In the wake of the Gulf War of 1990–91 the U.S. emerged as the dominant power in the region. In a throwback to the era of British imperialism, the strongest U.S. bond has been formed with the ministates of the GCC, where Washington had established a permanent military infrastructure. The U.S. Fifth Fleet was based in Bahrain, and a major airbase was built at Al Udeid in Qatar. Military equipment was prepositioned throughout the region, including Kuwait, Oman and the UAE. Saudi Arabia did not have a formal defense agreement with the U.S. due to public sensitivity but allowed Washington the use of its bases to maintain the no-fly zone in Iraq. When Secretary of State Baker outlined his postwar goals to Congress in February 1991, he said that Iran could play a role in future security arrangements. But this did not happen, nor was the "Damascus Declaration," issued in March, which called for Egyptian and Syrian troops to back up GCC forces, ever implemented.

In place of the balance-of-power strategy the U.S. had followed during the Iran-Iraq War, the Clinton Administration (1993–2001) introduced a new policy in May 1993, dubbed dual containment, which sought to pressure both Iran and Iraq and exclude them from regional affairs. The U.S. maintained that it accepted the Iranian revolution and harbored no hostility to Islam per se. But it accused Iran of supporting terrorism by inciting and funding groups violently opposed to Israel (including Hamas and Hezbollah), and assassinating Iranian dissidents abroad. Some government officials insisted that they had good evidence that Iran had a hand in the deadly bombing of the U.S. military barracks in Dhahran, Saudi Arabia, in June 1996. In addition, the U.S. charged that Iran was trying to acquire WMDs, was engaging in a buildup of conventional weapons, abused human rights and opposed the peace process.

The Clinton Administration felt that positive inducements such as trade and aid would not work with Iran. The U.S. sought instead to deny Tehran the military capabilities (by imposing strict export controls) and financial resources to carry out its policies. It pledged to contain Iran unilaterally, if need be, although it tried hard to persuade its allies to assist in this effort. In the spring of 1995, the U.S. prohibited an agreement between the U.S. oil company Conoco and Iran to develop two offshore oil fields in the Persian Gulf, and signed a sweeping order outlawing practically all trade with Iran. In August 1996, a new law (the Iran-Libya Sanctions Act, or ILSA) imposed sanctions on foreign companies that invest more than $40 million (later reduced to $20 million) to help develop Iran's oil and gas fields. Dual containment neither modified the behavior nor changed the government of Iran or Iraq, and, by 1998, it had effectively been abandoned. As for ILSA, with one exception it has never been implemented, due to objections from U.S. allies. After the removal of its applicability to

Libya in 2006, the name was changed to the Iran Sanctions Act (ISA), and it was invoked for the first time against an Iranian company in Switzerland in October 2010.

The Khatami years: missed opportunities

The U.S. responded positively if cautiously to the election of President Khatami in 1997. The old rhetoric labeling Iran as a "rogue" or "outlaw" state was shelved. In an important policy statement on June 17, 1998, Secretary of State Madeleine Albright urged Iran to join the U.S. in drawing up "a road map leading to normal relations." In March 2000, she went as far as any American official has gone in making a qualified apology for the U.S. role in overthrowing the Mossadeq government in 1953. Assassinations of Iranian dissidents in Europe ended, although Iranian hostility to the peace process continued. The U.S. attempt to engage Iran, unfortunately, did not succeed, and President Clinton left office without a policy breakthrough.

Policy toward Iraq

Although Iran was an irritant, both President Clinton and Bush II regarded Iraq as the real regional menace. Ten years after the allied defeat of Iraq had defused the immediate threat to Kuwait, the continued presence of Saddam was impoverishing and demoralizing Iraqi society and compromising the region's long-term security. The U.S. tried to contain Baghdad through UN sanctions, by regular inspections and monitoring by UNSCOM, and by enforcing no-fly zones in the north and south. After confrontations that led to U.S. military strikes in 1993, 1996 and 1998, in its last two years the Clinton Administration tried to avoid further military engagement. The Iraq Liberation Act, signed into law in October 1998, committed the U.S. to "support a transition to democracy in Iraq." The act provided nearly $100 million to fund the Iraqi opposition, and called on the U.S. to seek the removal of Saddam and replace his regime with a democratic form of government. This was to be a project for Bush II.

Whereas U.S. policy for a decade after the Gulf War was to maintain the status quo, the younger Bush opted for major change by waging a preventive war to oust Saddam. Administration policy on Iraq, Iran and indeed the entire Middle East, was influenced above all by the attacks of September 11, 2001, which highlighted the dangers of terrorism and WMDs.

After 9/11, the Bush Administration began laying the groundwork for wars in Afghanistan and Iraq. The attack on the Taliban began almost immediately, but it took two years to prepare public opinion to accept the necessity of another war against Iraq. Bush and his top advisers charged Iraq with carrying out a WMD program, although proof was debatable. (The consensus of experts before the war was that Iraq did have biological and chemical weapons, but there was disagreement about the state of its nuclear program.) A key charge was that Iraq was cooperating with terrorists, specifically al-Qaeda, and might transfer lethal weapons to them. A later justification for war was that introducing a democratic government in Baghdad would change political dynamics in the Middle East by spreading democracy. The idea that oil-rich Iraq could pay for the war was sometimes invoked, although this later proved to be illusory.

One troubling aspect of the march to war was the politicization of intelligence: "There is no doubt that the president and leading figures in the Administration 'cherry-picked' the intelligence in order to present the most lurid and frightening case about Iraqi capabilities and intentions, particularly on the nuclear and terrorist issues," according to Professor Gause. Unlike the case in 1990–91, the UN did not authorize the use of force against Iraq. However, Congress did so in October 2002, and the war was ultimately launched on March 20, 2003.

In the aftermath of 9/11, the U.S. was able to work with Iran to evict the Taliban and install the Karzai government in Afghanistan. Any goodwill and cooperation, however, was cut short by President Bush's designation of Iran as part of an "axis of evil" in his January 2002 State of the Union address. (Iran's inclusion was prompted by the discovery of shipborne weapons it was supposedly supplying to the Palestinian Authority.) Iran was accused of seeking to acquire nuclear weapons, obstructing the Arab-Israeli peace process, supporting terrorism and violating human rights. The Administration insisted that Iran give up any enrichment or reprocessing activity on its soil, but did not have enough support to bring Iran before the UN Security Council to impose sanctions. The U.S. let the Europeans, especially Britain, France and Germany (the EU-3), play a lead role in conducting negotiations over the nuclear issue.

The Obama Administration

When Obama took office in January 2009, he inherited long-running wars in Iraq and Afghanistan, a dysfunctional state in Pakistan, a failing Arab-Israeli peace process and an inability to bring Iran's nuclear program under control. All of this was a tall order for someone not known for expertise on foreign affairs, who was eager to work on domestic issues.

Two legacies of the Bush II presidency were widespread opposition to the wars it had started, and a perceived U.S. bias against Muslims. Obama quickly moved to repair the American image abroad. In an early interview with Al Arabiya, an Arabic-language channel based in Dubai, Obama sought to persuade Muslims that "the Americans are not your enemy." He also tried hard to win over Iranian leaders. Obama's message congratulating Iranians on their New Year (*No Ruz*) on March 20, 2009, stunned listeners by offering a "new beginning" and came close to ruling out a military strike against Iran, saying "this process will not be advanced by threats." He sought instead "engagement that is honest and grounded in mutual respect." This prompted an unprecedented response from Ayatollah Khamenei, who said, "should you change, our behavior will change, too."

In a major address in Cairo, Egypt, on June 4, 2009, Obama said he had come to seek "a new beginning between the U.S. and Muslims around the world; one based upon mutual interest and mutual respect, and one based upon the truth that America and Islam are not exclusive and need not be in competition…." He said, "America is not—and never will be—at war with Islam. We will, however,

PETE SOUZA/WHITE HOUSE/HANDOUT/CNP/CORBIS

President Barack Obama waves to the audience at Cairo University in Cairo, Egypt.

relentlessly confront violent extremists who pose a grave threat to our security...." He continued to hold out hope of discussing issues with Iran "without preconditions and on the basis of mutual respect."

But a year into his presidency, much of the initial goodwill had dissipated. According to polls administered by Zogby International and Shibley Telhami, professor of international relations at the University of Maryland, in June and July 2010, 63% of Arabs were discouraged about U.S. policies, regional views were more positive of Iran's nuclear program, and Obama's disapproval rating went from 23% in 2009 to 62% in 2010. A follow-up Zogby poll taken in May and June 2011 found that U.S. popularity had plummeted in the region, due to a failure to meet expectations and lack of progress in the peace process.

How the Obama Administration handles the aftermath of the uprising in Egypt, and its reverberations in neighboring states, will surely define its legacy in the Middle East. One problem is noted by Professor Telhami: "Today, our closest institutional relationships in the Arab world, driven by strategic U.S. priorities, are military to military, intelligence to intelligence, security service to security service. These agencies are the anchors of repression in the region, regardless of who rules at the top. Given that repression now appears to be failing, this is the moment for a bigger assessment of U.S. policy in the region—beyond what happens in Egypt."

From engagement to pressure

The first year in office Obama tried to reach out to Tehran, but by early 2010 he shifted from engagement to a "pressure track," in the words of then Defense Secretary Robert Gates. Efforts to engage Iran did not elicit a positive response from Tehran, which was preoccupied by the widespread protests that followed the Iranian presidential election. Many suspected that the Ahmadinejad government sought to bolster its legitimacy by invoking the U.S. as an enemy. Critics faulted Obama for not promoting issues of human rights and democracy more strongly, and for being slow to criticize the Tehran government's brutal crackdown in the summer of 2009 (Obama said it would be counterproductive for the U.S. to be seen as meddling).

By the fall of 2009, however, things had changed. In October, following revelations of a secret enrichment plant under construction near Qom, Iranian and American negotiators met publicly in Geneva for the first time since the revolution. They struck a deal in which Iran would transfer a major portion of its LEU outside the country (building confidence that it was not trying to weaponize), in return for fuel rods it could use in a medical reactor. It appeared that the U.S. had given up on its previous redline and would now permit Iranian enrichment. What had been hailed as a breakthrough deal soon fell apart, however, among political infighting in Tehran and fears that the U.S. had bested Iran in the negotiations.

The U.S. position then hardened, and Obama's rhetoric changed. In his acceptance speech for the Nobel Peace Prize in Oslo, Norway, on December 10, he said, "Those regimes that break the rules must be held accountable. Sanctions must exact a real price. Intransigence must be met with increased pressure...." In the spring of 2010, the U.S. worked hard to line up international support for a fourth round of UN sanctions, which were passed in June. It was widely acknowledged, however, that these would not force Iran to give up enrichment, and many worried that the U.S. was just going through the motions to help justify an eventual strike. With the opposition Green Movement in Iran fading and little likelihood that the Iranian government would cooperate, the U.S. was left without a viable Iran policy. In August 2011 the State Department repeated its designation of Iran as "the most active state sponsor of terrorism in 2010," as it has annually since 1984.

Given its limited options for affecting events inside the country, the U.S. did what it could, such as stepping up broadcasts to Iran and authorizing the export to Iran of online services like instant messaging, chat and photo sharing to get around internet censorship. The U.S. also funded a secret "Democracy Program" starting in 2006 aimed at regime change in Iran, with most money going to broadcast outlets such as Radio Farda, Voice of America and Radio Free Europe. Iranian reformers such as Nobel Laureate Shirin Ebady and dissident Akbar Ganji have urged Washington not to appropriate money for civil society or opposition groups in Iran, as it only delegitimizes their cause and puts them in danger. The U.S. is suspected of providing covert support for disaffected ethnic groups, such as the Kurds, Arabs and Baluchis, in hopes of destabilizing the Tehran government, but this is hard to verify.

In the most spectacular and successful project (publicly denied), the U.S. was suspected of secretly working with Israel to develop the Stuxnet computer worm, which infected and disabled computers in Iranian nuclear plants between June 2009 and May 2010. (As of September 2011 some 8,000 centrifuges had been installed at Natanz but only about 5,800 were enriching uranium.) By seriously harming these computers, the perpetrators of this attack achieved through cyberwarfare what would have been the aim of a military strike. This significantly reduced pressure for an attack and put time on the nuclear clock.

Arab Spring: the U.S. response

Calibrating the U.S. response to the events of the Arab Spring has been one of the greatest foreign policy challenges for the Obama Administration. Repeatedly, the U.S. has been forced to take sides between a popular uprising demanding democracy and the autocratic rulers it had long worked with who ensured security and "stability." In the case of Tunisia, the first successful revolt, few U.S. interests were at stake and it was not difficult to cut ties to the leader. Egypt, however, was a different story. President Mubarak had been a close U.S. ally for 30 years and had kept the peace with Israel. After equivocating at first, eventually the U.S. voiced support for the demonstrators and accepted that Mubarak had to go.

President Obama's response to the spreading upheaval, however, was inconsistent. "Obama's ultimate position, it seemed, was to talk like an idealist while acting like a realist," wrote Ryan Lizza in *The New Yorker*. The U.S. stood for democracy, and this guided its policy in Tunisia and Egypt. However, events in the Gulf were a different matter. When confronted with the uprising in Bahrain, the U.S. held back on criticism of the ruling family due to the island's strategic importance. The U.S. urged the ruling Al Khalifa family to find a peaceful solution, but this advice was disregarded. In the case of Saudi Arabia, where there were some demonstrations, the U.S. was notably silent and supportive of the ruling family. The Al Sa'ud were greatly angered at the forced departure of Mubarak, and feared that the U.S. would abandon them next. Israel also was distressed at the loss of its longtime partner for peace.

U.S. statements, while not going so far as to accept GCC claims that Iran was behind the events in Bahrain, did warn Iran to stop meddling or taking advantage of the turmoil there or in other Arab states. After major demonstrations in Tehran on February 14, the U.S. strongly took the side of the protesters, in contrast to its restrained reaction during the 2009 uprising.

The U.S. was criticized for not having a consistent response to the Arab awakening—rather, tailoring one for each country. In general it was opposed to regime change, but urged rulers to avoid violence and make reforms. Democracy was not required in the GCC states, especially Bahrain, where protesters were encouraged to negotiate. The Administration reportedly worked behind the scenes to get the government to pull back its forces and also tried to prevent Saudi Arabia from deploying troops, to no avail. "Starting with Bahrain, the administration has moved a few notches toward emphasizing stability over majority rule," a U.S. official told the *Wall Street Journal* in early March.

In a major speech on the Middle East on May 19, Obama tried to break the stalemate in the Arab-Israeli peace talks, but he had little to say about the Gulf. He assured protesters in Bahrain that the U.S. supported them: "The only way forward is for the government and opposition to engage in a dialogue, and you can't have a real dialogue when parts of the peaceful opposition are in jail." He announced, "it will be the policy of the U.S. to promote reform across the region, and to support transitions to democracy." Notable is what Obama left out of the speech: Saudi Arabia was not mentioned, there was no support for democracy in Bahrain, no mention of talks with Iran nor the path forward in Iraq. While employing soaring rhetoric, Obama did not outline a coherent policy for the region.

Arms sales and bases

The U.S. understands that it has an obligation to protect its allies in the GCC states from Iran. In early 2010 Washington bolstered their defenses, deploying Patriot missiles to Qatar, the UAE, Bahrain and Kuwait (Saudi Arabia already had them). This aimed to deter an Iranian attack, reassure the Arab Gulf states, and mollify the Israelis. In a speech in Doha, Qatar, in February 2010, Secretary of State Clinton reminded Arab states that they should not sit back and rely on the U.S., but needed to help Washington achieve its policy goals for Iran. In November 2010, following required notification to Congress, the Pentagon began to carry out the largest arms sale ever to Saudi Arabia, a $60 billion package including F-15 fighter jets, Apache helicopters and Black Hawk helicopters.

An important issue is the future of the U.S. base in Bahrain, where the Fifth Fleet has been stationed since 1995. With some 30 warships and 30,000 sailors, the Fifth Fleet patrols the Gulf, as well as the Arabian Sea, the Red Sea and parts of the Indian Ocean. It keeps the sea lanes open, ensuring the flow of oil, fights piracy and keeps an eye on Iran. It also contributes about $150 million to the local

U.S. Navy Capt. Ted R. Williams welcomes the King of Bahrain, Hamad bin Isa Al Khalifa, aboard the USS *Dwight D. Eisenhower*.

economy every year. It is a critical part of the U.S. force structure and until now Bahrain has been a reliable host. In September 2011 it was revealed that the U.S. and Bahrain had secretly extended their defense cooperation agreement in 2002, and it now runs to 2016.

However, some are beginning to question whether this base is necessary, especially in light of the political instability. Could it be moved elsewhere? The U.S. also has military installations in Oman, the UAE, Qatar and Kuwait. The cost of moving would be high, as facilities in Bahrain were built over many years, and it is doubtful whether any other GCC state would welcome the U.S. Also, critical minesweepers would have to be relocated. Should there be a regime change in Bahrain, a move could become necessary. According to Toby C. Jones of Rutgers University, the fleet could become a political liability and should be eliminated. He maintains that the U.S. has other military and naval facilities outside the Gulf that could respond quickly there, and "most importantly, its presence enables regional allies to act recklessly." He no longer sees a need for a major military presence in the Gulf, and he notes that regional allies do not need U.S. protection to sell their oil. Clearly, the debate on the future U.S. force structure in the region is just beginning.

Israel and the Persian Gulf

For many years, U.S. policymakers tried to separate policy for Israel and the Palestinians from issues in the Gulf, but in the Middle East, everything is connected and this ultimately proved to be impossible. Support by Gulf Arabs for the Palestinians is strong, at least rhetorically, which has curtailed their relations with Israel. The linkage became obvious in October 1973 after many Arab states (and all Gulf oil producers except Oman and Iran) imposed an oil embargo in retaliation for U.S. support for Israel in the war. Much later, following the allied air attack on Iraq in January 1991, Hussein responded by aiming some 40 Scud missiles at Israel.

Because of hostility to the current government in Iran on the part of Israel and the Gulf monarchs, it has sometimes been suggested that they could form a common front to oppose Iran. However, this seems fanciful as long as the peace process is stalled. The Gulf states already have discreet links with Israel, notes Sultan Sooud Al Qassemi, an analyst in the UAE. Israeli officials are known to have visited Oman and Qatar, and there were Israeli trade offices in Doha and Muscat, now closed. Ironically, the leadership in Israel and the Gulf monarchies found themselves on the same side in backing Mubarak against the anti-government protests.

Clearly, advancing the peace process can pay dividends in the Gulf. The President seems to have accepted the warning by General David Petraeus that lack of progress in the Palestinian-Israeli arena endangers U.S. troops in the region.

U.S. Administration support for Israel has traditionally been very strong, especially in the run-up to national elections, and pro-Israeli lobby groups such as the American Israel Public Affairs Committee (AIPAC) work hard to maintain congressional support. But Israel's interests may not be identical to those of the U.S., and their intelligence assessments of Iran have often differed, notably in the time required for Iran to produce a weapon. Pressure by the Israeli government for the U.S. to get tough on Iran and consider military options has led to strains with Washington, which has tried to forestall any unilateral Israeli attack.

The nuclear issue

Perhaps the most difficult issue is Iran's nuclear program. It is quite possible that no decision has been made by Iran to produce a weapon; rather, it may be trying to master the technology so that if a decision were made to weaponize, it could quickly do so. A possible solution has been evident to experts for some time. As Professor Sick observed in testimony to the (House) Committee on International Relations in February 2005, the best course might be to offer Iran incentives to put limits on its program. Sick suggests that "the outline of a realistic outcome to the negotiations would involve a combination of a contained, monitored enrichment program and economic and political integration of Iran with the West. The fear of losing the benefits of integration, together with intensive inspections and controls over fissile material, could inhibit the temptations of some in Iran to use the enrichment program to acquire nuclear weapons. This is not a bargain that is likely to be welcomed either by Iran or the U.S., but it may be the least worst outcome."

This wisdom has been challenged by others as years of fruitless negotiations have made no progress in curtailing the program. David Albright and Paul Brannan of the Institute for Science and International Security in Washington cautioned in June 2011 that "without a major change in behavior, accepting Iranian enrichment merely serves as a self-defeating 'red-line' that Iran could step over whenever it chose.... After reaching a hard-won agreement, the international community may be hesitant to scuttle the entire agreement over infractions, and the controversy over Iran's transgressions could soon pass."

What, then, should the U.S. do? It is clear that in light of the most recent U.S. and Israeli estimates, there is still time to negotiate since no breakout is imminent. Policy analyst Graham Allison concludes that "the bottom line for American policy is that the menu of feasible options has shrunk. Every option available at this point requires living with an Iran that knows how to enrich uranium. Continued denial of this truth is self-delusion. The central policy question becomes: what combination of arrangements, inside and outside Iran, has the best chance of persuading it to stop short of a nuclear bomb?"

Missing expertise

The prerequisite to formulating effective policies is accurate information, which in the case of both Iraq and Iran has been seriously lacking or else simply disregarded. The governments of the U.S. and Iran have become the prisoners of their own rhetoric, often abetted by the news media. "Both sides are caught in narratives developed not only to antagonize one another, but also to appease their respective domestic audiences," according to Professor Farhi. Even at the height of the cold war, the U.S. had an embassy in Moscow and carried on a dialogue on many subjects. If the U.S. can enjoy normal relations with former adversaries such as the Soviet Union or Vietnam, it should be possible to do so with Iran in spite of memories of the hostage crisis. In the absence of an official dialogue, behind-the-scenes, "track two" discussions that came to a halt under Ahmadinejad could resume. Confidence-building measures which have proven effective in other parts of the world are long overdue for this region. Iran bashing has predictably been popular in Congress, and congressional and Israeli opposition to dealing with Iran has been a major reason Administrations have approached normalization gingerly. Today the Iranian exile community in the U.S. is taking a more active political role in hope of influencing policy.

A whole generation has come of age in Iran without any personal knowledge of the country its government likes to refer to as "the Great Satan." On the eve of the revolution, in the 1978–79 academic year, over 45,000 Iranian students (about half of all studying abroad) were enrolled in U.S. schools. In 2009–10, only 4,731 were studying in the U.S., according to the Institute of International

Education. The risk is increasing that new generations of Americans and Iranians will forget the past legacy of cooperation and become permanently estranged. In a much-appreciated gesture, in May 2011 the State Department eased visa regulations for Iranian students.

There is now a serious lack of U.S. expertise on Iran that has hindered relations, according to Ambassador John Limbert, a former Iranian hostage. Few Americans have been to Iran in the past 30 years, and diplomats with experience in Iran have now mostly retired. In the 1980s and 1990s the State Department did not even train Persian speakers. The Modern Language Association of America reported that in the fall of 2009 about 35,000 Americans were studying Arabic and only 2,800 Persian in all forms, whereas 865,000 were studying Spanish. "The point is that the U.S. should be talking to the Islamic Republic not because doing so is easy or even likely to produce immediate and positive results, but because both sides might find significant common interests in doing so," according to Limbert.

Bomb Iran?

As frustration in dealing with Tehran has built in the U.S. and other countries, the efficacy of a military strike against Iran's nuclear sites has been widely debated. Some believe that an attack could be as successful as the Israeli raids on the reactors under construction in Iraq (1981) and Syria (2007). Reuel Marc Gerecht, a former CIA analyst, argued in July 2010 that "although dangerous for Israel, a preventive strike remains the most effective answer to the possibility of Khamenei and the Revolutionary Guards having nuclear weapons…; an Israeli bombardment remains the only conceivable means of derailing or seriously delaying Iran's nuclear program and—equally important—traumatizing Iran." Gerecht suggests that in the aftermath of such an attack, it is likely that Iranians would rise up against their leadership.

Top U.S. military officials have advised against this and sought to prevent a unilateral Israeli strike. Secretary Gates argued, "Another war in the Middle East is the last thing we need. I believe it would be disastrous on a number of levels," and Admiral Mike Mullen, Chairman of the Joint Chiefs of Staff, also expressed serious reservations about any attack. Many see this as a bad idea that might set back Iran by a few years, but would lead to unforeseen and serious consequences in the region, and could put American troops in jeopardy. Iran's nuclear facilities are dispersed and hidden, and it is unlikely that all locations could be hit. Hard-liners would take control of the government, as they did during the Iran-Iraq War, and the pro-American people of Iran would rapidly turn against the U.S. The disadvantages of such a military option would far outweigh its advantages.

Sanctions so far have not achieved the desired goal—forcing Iran to abandon any nuclear weapons program—although Stuart Levey, the undersecretary for terrorism and financial intelligence, maintained in December 2010 that "Iran is feeling the pressure of sanctions as never before." But as long as oil prices are high and China retains its extensive economic ties with Iran, their effectiveness will be curtailed. It seems very unlikely that Obama will authorize a war with Iran in the remainder of his term.

Conclusion

At a time of bitter political infighting in Iran, the U.S. should not expect quick progress on negotiations. After decades of estrangement, there is little trust on either side. As Professor Sick suggests, "the U.S. can continue treating Iran as a permanent enemy to be confronted and isolated, thereby perpetuating the policies of the past three Administrations. Or it can begin treating the Islamic Republic as a potentially 'normal' power—subject to the usual blandishments of carrots and sticks. This accepts that Tehran has the capacity not only to annoy us but perhaps also to help ease some of Washington's worst dilemmas in the region." When talks resume, they should not focus solely on the nuclear program to the exclusion of other issues; fruitful conversations, for example, might take place on the situation in Iraq and Afghanistan, where the U.S. needs Iranian cooperation to achieve smooth withdrawals, not to mention security in the Gulf. Hopefully, the U.S. and Iran can break the historic pattern of never being able to reciprocate the other's advances.

A major improvement in the regional security situation probably will not come, however, until U.S.-Iran relations are normalized. After

30 years of estrangement, bilateral ties have reached a new low, especially following the postelection crackdown that began in the summer of 2009. In the long run—however long this is—ties will improve, because it is in Iran's interest and is what most Iranians want. Iranians are very proud of their country and its heritage, and are pained that their country is regarded as a pariah state. They want to rejoin the world. When this happens, the Iranian dream of a regional security agreement may be realized.

$$\Rightarrow \circ \Leftarrow$$

The relationship between Americans and Iranians has been a story of friendship, betrayal and many missed opportunities for reconciliation. The Iranian people clearly want to strengthen ties with the U.S.; for Americans, the imperative is less clear. Momentum for such a change, though, must come from the top, which does not seem likely at present. A normalization of relations between the U.S. and Iran, and Iran's reintegration into the world as a "normal" nation, will still take some time.

As for Iraq, although American troops are leaving, it is likely that the U.S. will remain closely involved militarily, economically and politically for some time. The question for many Americans is, after over eight years of war, has it been worth it? In considering the legacy of the Iraq War, the *Los Angeles Times* editorialized, "The war can be considered a victory in just one sense: It removed Hussein. In all other respects, the war in Iraq was a misadventure that compromised U.S. national interests, and was too costly for too little return."

Finally, the question of whether a new Middle East will emerge in the wake of widespread demands for democracy in the Arab states, and the advent of new governments (so far) in Egypt and Tunisia, has already had consequences in the Gulf. The U.S. may revive the "freedom agenda" advocated by Bush and rethink its ties to local autocrats, although this will not be easy for Washington policymakers. It is certain that the Gulf and safeguarding its petroleum resources will continue to be central U.S. policy concerns.

Talking It Over

A Note for Students and Discussion Groups

This issue of the HEADLINE SERIES, like its predecessors, is published for every serious reader who takes an interest in the subject. Many of our readers will be in classrooms, seminars or community discussion groups. Particularly with them in mind, we present below some discussion questions—suggested as a starting point only—and references for further reading, as well as pertinent online resources.

Discussion Questions

The Persian Gulf region has undergone an accelerated period of modernization, facilitated by large energy revenues. How has this process placed pressure on traditional social and political systems? (Consider, for instance, the role of modern technology, such as social media and the internet, in the 2009 Iranian election and the 2011 "Arab Spring" popular demonstrations.) How have the countries of the Persian Gulf responded to these pressures? To what extent do governmental responses follow historical patterns?

How is the U.S. interest in regional security compromised by the prospect of a nuclear Iran? How should the U.S. balance its interest in opposing nuclear proliferation with its need for energy? How much pressure should the U.S. put on its allies regarding human rights and political liberalization?

What is the U.S. legacy in the Persian Gulf? How has U.S. intervention or interference—with the Iranian revolution, the Iraqi invasion of Kuwait, and the ousting of Saddam Hussein from Iraq—affected the Gulf? What have been the costs and benefits of intervention in the region?

Political rivalries exist among countries of the Persian Gulf, yet there are also religious, linguistic and ethnic identities that transcend national boundaries. What is the balance of power between governments and transborder religious, ethnic and linguistic populations?

How has the export of petroleum resources shaped the development of the Persian Gulf and the relations of Persian Gulf nations with each other and the Western world? What attitudes and practices have been least affected by modernization? How does the "resource curse" offer opportunities as well as dangers to the region?

Relations between the U.S. and Iran have been tense since the 1978–79 revolution. How does each side regard the other, and what would be required for both sides to reconcile?

Annotated Reading List

Abrahamian, Ervand, *A History of Modern Iran.* Cambridge, England, Cambridge University Press, 2008. An authoritative overview of the 20th century.

Ansari, Ali M., *Modern Iran: The Pahlavis and After,* 2nd ed. Harlow, England, Pearson Education Limited, 2007. An important interpretative history of modern Iran.

Cottrell, Alvin J., ed., *The Persian Gulf States: A General Survey.* Baltimore, The Johns Hopkins University Press, 1980. A classic one-volume reference to the Persian Gulf, especially strong on history and society.

Davidson, Christopher M., *Dubai: The Vulnerability of Success.* New York, Columbia University Press, 2008. A detailed and critical study of Dubai's evolution from a free port to the most successful city in the Gulf.

Davis, Eric, *Memories of State: Politics, History, and Collective Identity in Modern Iraq.* Berkeley, University of California Press, 2005. An original examination of the relationship between state power, historical memory and authoritarian rule in modern Iraq.

Esposito, John L., *Islam: The Straight Path*, 4th ed. New York, Oxford University Press, 2010. The most widely used introductory text on the faith, belief and practice of Islam.

Fernea, Elizabeth Warnock, *Guests of the Sheik: An Ethnography of an Iraqi Village.* New York, Doubleday, 1965. Thoroughly delightful and well-written, this book is a classic account of a two-year stay in a tiny rural village in southern Iraq in the 1950s.

Freedman, Lawrence, and Karsh, Efraim, *The Gulf Conflict 1990-1991: Diplomacy and War in the New World Order.* London, Faber and Faber, 1993. An authoritative account of Iraq's occupation of Kuwait and its expulsion by a coalition of western and Arab forces.

Gause, F. Gregory, III, *The International Relations of the Persian Gulf.* New York, Cambridge University Press, 2010. The best one-volume treatment, covering the wars which have reshaped the region from 1980 to the present. Especially strong on the current Iraq War.

Heard-Bey, Frauke, *From Trucial States to United Arab Emirates.* Dubai, UAE, Motivate Publishing, 2005. The standard history of the UAE, describing traditional tribal society and its evolution into the modern state.

Held, Colbert C., and Cummings, John Thomas, *Middle East Patterns: Places, Peoples, and Politics*, 5th ed. Boulder, Colo.: Westview Press, 2010. A comprehensive geography of the Middle East, with much information on the Gulf states.

Al-Hijji, Yacoub Yusuf, *Kuwait and the Sea: A Brief Social and Economic History,* trans. Fahad Bishara. London, Arabian Publishing, 2010. A fascinating book by Kuwait's leading expert in the country's maritime history.

International Crisis Group, "Popular Protest in North Africa and the Middle East (VIII): Bahrain's Rocky Road to Reform." Middle East/North Africa Report No. 111, July 28, 2011. Review of the recent upheaval which urges a direct dialogue leading to political reform. Available at: http://www.crisisgroup.org/en/regions/middle-east-north-africa/iran-gulf/bahrain/111-popular-protest-in-north-africa-and-the-middle-east-viii-bahrains-rocky-road-to-reform.aspx

Izady, Mehrdad R., *The Kurds: A Concise Handbook.* Washington, D.C., Taylor & Francis, 1992. The best one-volume introduction to the subject.

Janardhan, N., *Boom amid Gloom: The Spirit of Possibility in the 21st Century Gulf.* Reading, England, Ithaca Press, 2011. One of the best political analysts of the Gulf, based in Dubai, examines how the oil boom of 2003–2008 has affected the development of the GCC states.

Kamrava, Mehran, ed., *International Politics of the Persian Gulf.* Syracuse, NY, Syracuse University Press, 2011. An up-to-date assessment of the causes and consequences of the security challenges facing the Persian Gulf states.

Kéchichian, Joseph A., *Power and Succession in Arab Monarchies: A Reference Guide.* Boulder, Colo., Lynne Rienner, 2008. A useful and detailed profile of the royal families in the GCC states.

Limbert, John W., *Negotiating with Iran: Wrestling the Ghosts of History.* Washington, D.C., U.S. Institute of Peace Press, 2009. Sage advice from one of the leading U.S. experts on Iran.

Long, David E., and Maisel, Sebastian, *The Kingdom of Saudi Arabia,* 2nd ed. Gainesville, University Press of Florida, 2010. An excellent general survey of Saudi Arabia, based on extensive firsthand experience.

Louër, Laurence, *Transnational Shia Politics: Religious and Political Networks in the Gulf.* New York, Columbia University Press, 2008. An original examination of the origins and present status of Shi'i networks in Iraq, Saudi Arabia, Kuwait and Bahrain.

Marr, Phebe, *The Modern History of Iraq,* 3rd ed. Boulder, Colo., Westview Press, 2011. Leading historian places the present crises in historical perspective—a comprehensive and up-to-the-minute political, economic and social history.

Molavi, Afshin, *The Soul of Iran: A Nation's Journey to Freedom,* rev. ed. New York, W.W. Norton, 2005. A remarkable portrait of contemporary Iran by journalist who traveled throughout the country during the Khatami years.

Munif, Abdelrahman, *Cities of Salt,* trans. Peter Theroux. New York, Vintage Books, 1989. A novel, set in Saudi Arabia, that sensitively chronicles the profound changes caused by the discovery of oil.

Nasr, Vali, *The Shia Revival: How Conflicts within Islam Will Shape the Future.* New York: W.W. Norton, 2007. Excellent background on the struggle between the Shi'i and Sunnis. Nasr argues that the Shi'i Crescent—stretching from Lebanon and Syria through the Gulf to Iraq and Iran, terminating in Pakistan and India—has gathered strength in the post-Saddam era.

O'Donnell, Terence, *Garden of the Brave in War: Recollections of Iran.* Washington, D.C., Mage Publishers, 2003. Beautiful memoir by an American who lived in rural Iran in the 1960s; full of colorful characters.

Onley, James, "Britain and the Gulf Shaikhdoms, 1820–1971: The Politics of Protection." Doha, Center for International and Regional Studies, Georgetown University School of Foreign Service in Qatar, 2009, *Occasional Paper* No. 4. An important reevaluation of how Britain maintained its empire in the Gulf by relying on native elites. Available at: http://cirs.georgetown.edu/publications/papers/100764.html

Palmer, Michael A., *Guardians of the Gulf: A History of America's Expanding Role in the Persian Gulf, 1833-1992.* New York, Free Press, 1992. Standard reference on the historical connection of the U.S. to the Gulf.

Parsi, Trita, *Treacherous Alliance: The Secret Dealings of Israel, Iran, and the United States.* New Haven, Conn., Yale University Press, 2008. Traces the shifting relations among the three states from 1948 to the present.

Peck, Malcolm C., *Historical Dictionary of the Gulf Arab States,* 2nd. ed. Lanham, Md., Scarecrow Press, 2008. Convenient reference on all the GCC states except Saudi Arabia.

Potter, Lawrence G., ed., *The Persian Gulf in History.* New York, Palgrave Macmillan, 2009. An overview of the history of the Gulf from pre-Islamic times to the present, emphasizing the region's unique identity and strong connection to the Indian Ocean world.

———, and Sick, Gary, eds., *Iran, Iraq, and the Legacies of War.* New York, Palgrave Macmillan, 2004. Examines the historical relationship of Iran and Iraq, the effect of the Iran-Iraq War on the regional states, and background to current disputes.

Al-Rasheed, Madawi, *A History of Saudi Arabia,* 2nd ed. Cambridge, England, Cambridge University Press, 2010. An excellent overview by leading Saudi historian, including the challenges the state faces in the 21st century.

Slavin, Barbara, *Bitter Friends, Bosom Enemies: Iran, the U.S., and the Twisted Path to Confrontation.* New York, St. Martin's Press, 2009. Washington journalist reviews the troubled relations between the two states, emphasizing the many missed opportunities for rapprochement.

Ulrichsen, Kristian Coates, *Insecure Gulf: The End of Certainty and the Transition to the Post-Oil Era.* London, Hurst, 2011. An important and incisive new study on the evolution of Gulf security that considers future threats to the stability of the Gulf, including demographic, economic and environmental factors.

Zahlan, Rosemarie Said, *The Making of the Modern Gulf States: Kuwait, Bahrain, Qatar, the United Arab Emirates and Oman,* revised and updated ed. London, Ithaca Press, 1998. The creation and evolution of the GCC states as told by a leading historian of the region.

Online Resources

http://gulf2000.columbia.edu Based at Columbia University, the Gulf/2000 Project is the largest research and documentation project on the Gulf states. This Web site provides links to many resources and original maps of the region.

https://www.cia.gov/library/publications/the-world-factbook The World Factbook is a standard reference for all countries in the world which is continuously updated and contains much useful information.

http://www.prb.org/Publications/Datasheets/2011/world-population-data-sheet.aspx The Population Reference Bureau annually publishes its World Population Data Sheet, a reliable survey of many important indicators, including population, urbanization, income, etc.

http://internetworldstats.com Internet World Stats tracks and regularly updates statistics on internet usage in countries around the world.

http://www.eia.gov The Energy Information Administration, a U.S. government agency, pubishes forecasts and analyses of reserves and demand for petroleum resources around the world.

http://www.mesa.arizona.edu The Middle East Studies Association is the leading group for scholars interested in the Middle East. It holds a major conference in the fall and publishes a scholarly journal.

http://www.mei.edu The Middle East Institute in Washington, D.C. is the oldest scholarly center devoted to the region, holds frequent events and publishes *The Middle East Journal.*

http://cirs. georgetown.edu/publications/ The Center for International and Regional Studies in Doha, Qatar, holds an impressive lecture series and has published a number of excellent papers on the Gulf, all available free.

http://www.state.gov/r/pa/ei/bgn/ The *Background Notes* series of the U.S. State Department are regularly updated profiles of the land, people, history, government, economy, and foreign relations of the countries in the Gulf and throughout the world.